THE *THINKING CLEARLY* SERIES

Series editor: Clive Calver

The *Thinking Clearly* series sets out the main issues in a variety of important subjects. Written from a mainstream Christian standpoint, the series combines clear biblical teaching with up-to-date scholarship. Each of the contributors is an authority in his or her field. The series is written in straightforward everyday language, and each volume includes a range of practical applications and guidance for further reading.

The series has two main aims:
1. To help Christians understand their faith better
2. To show how Christian truths can illuminate matters of crucial importance in our society.

THE *THINKING CLEARLY* SERIES

Series Editor: Clive Calver

Thinking Clearly About The Uniqueness of Jesus

CHRIS WRIGHT

MONARCH

EVANGELICAL ALLIANCE
SCB PUBLISHERS

British Library Cataloguing Data
A catalogue record for this book is available
from the British Library.

ISBN 1 85424 347 0

Co-published with

The Evangelical Alliance,
Whitefield House, 186 Kennington Park Road,
London SE11 4BT

SCB Publishers Ltd
Cornelis Struik House, 80 McKenzie Street,
Cape Town 8001, South Africa
Reg no 04/02203/06

*Front cover photo: stained glass detail
courtesy of Glyn Simister Lewis*

Designed and produced by Bookprint Creative Services
P.O. Box 827, BN21 3YJ, England for
MONARCH PUBLICATIONS
Broadway House, The Broadway,
Crowborough, East Sussex, TN6 1HQ.
Printed in Great Britain.

For
Jonny and Emma

Contents

Preface

The origins of this book go back more than a decade. I was invited
by David Wenham, then editor of the theological students'
journal *Themelios* to contribute an article on a biblical
perspective on Christianity and other religions. This appeared in
Vol. 9.2 (Jan 1984). That led to an invitation from John Stott on
behalf of the London Institute for Contemporary Christianity,
now Christian Impact, to deliver a lecture there in April 1986 on
'The Uniqueness of Christ in the Context of Religious Pluralism'.
Both of these were combined to produce the first in the series of
All Nations Booklets, edited by Martin Goldsmith, *What's so
Unique about Jesus?* (Monarch, 1990). It is that booklet which
has been fully revised, expanded and updated to produce the
present volume in the *Thinking Clearly* series. I am grateful to all
the aforementioned friends for their part in an ongoing project,
and to Tony Collins of Monarch Publications for his enthusiastic
insistence on giving the work a fresh and enlarged lease of life,
and for his patience in waiting for the re-birth. As always, my
wife and family are to be thanked for their support in this as in all
my work, and the book is dedicated to the first of our sons to
marry and to the third daughter he has joyfully brought us.

Chris Wright
All Nations Christian College
October 1996

Introduction:

Welcome to the Supermarket!

Welcome to the Supermarket!

Walking into a British supermarket for the first time after several years of living in India turned out to be an unnerving experience. In India (when my family and I lived there) you could get either cornflakes or wheatflakes as breakfast cereals. The choice mattered little since they were made by the same people and tasted equally unappetising. So more often than not our family avoided both and either enjoyed a spicier Indian start to the day, or endured another morning of my homemade mixed cereal porridge with homemade buffalo milk yoghurt. But in the British supermarket the shelves of breakfast cereals stretched to a blurred horizon and the infinity of choice paralysed me. I postponed a decision by just counting the number of different brands. I gave up at forty-five and hadn't even reached the end of one row of shelves, and my trolley was still empty.

After a few visits to a supermarket, of course, you quickly learn to go straight for what you know you like and filter out the rest. You can't do a multiple-choice exam every time you go shopping. The supermarket mentality takes over: it doesn't really matter what you choose so long as you like it. The packaging is different, but inside the boxes, apart from the menagerie of stickers, pictures and terror-striking one-inch plastic monsters, they're all going to be much the same and meet the same needs. They're all fortified with extra vitamins and so long as you can visualise what

30 grams of them look like in a bowl, you've only got 75% of your adult daily intake of vitamins left to find for that day. None of them will fulfil claims to help you be a sports hero or a fashion model, but then none of them will leave you malnourished either. So none of them is right or wrong – except for you. Choose whatever suits your taste and preference. Or choose for the sake of the kids. Take your pick and move to the next row of shelves.

The supermarket mentality

The supermarket mentality has taken over more than our shopping habits. It has become the characteristic western way of approaching more important matters. It dominates moral attitudes. Whatever values you choose for your behaviour is a private matter and moral choices are only subjective preferences influenced by cultural, emotional or religious pressures (just as advertising or a demanding child may influence our choice of cereal). We don't accept standards any more; we choose our own values (or, more likely, we allow others to choose them for us and go along with the herd).

Similarly, the supermarket mentality dominates popular thinking about religion. For a long time ordinary people were fairly indifferent to the different brand names of Christian denominations. Whatever name was on the outside of the packaging, what you found inside a church was likely to be much the same as anywhere else, so you chose what suited you. Now it is no longer different denominations but different whole religions that compete on the supermarket shelves. But if it doesn't much matter whether you're a Methodist or an Anglican, why does it matter whether you're a Christian or a Hindu, a Muslim or a Buddhist?

In the midst of such plurality, is it still right to claim any special place for Christianity? Or to be more precise, can we still claim that Jesus Christ is unique, as only God and Saviour? The supermarket mentality says 'No' because its whole approach makes such a claim frankly implausible. You have to have healthy competition. You have to be free to choose, and choice will not tolerate a monopoly. All the breakfast cereals can make their different claims and advertise their special features, but any one of them which claimed to be the only one with any food value at all would be laughed off the shelves. A famous beer can claim to be 'probably' the best lager in the world, but if it claimed to be the *only* true lager in the world, imagine the protests!

The supermarket mentality sees everything as a commodity, and everybody as a consumer. Religions are fitted into the same picture: they have their brand names, their grand claims, and their marketing strategies. Religions indeed are not unlike the great supermarket giants, competing for a leading share of the market, concerned about gaining or losing customers, striving to be user-friendly, even talking about 'loyalty' (to a supermarket?!).

Not surprisingly, then, this supermarket mentality is very critical of Christians who make claims about their faith and about Jesus which appear to deny the validity of other religions. Arrogance and intolerance are the words commonly hurled at such a stance. In such a climate of opinion, how should Christians present their faith? Unfortunately, many Christians accept the supermarket approach and pretend it is evangelism: 'I have found that Jesus satisfies my needs, so why don't you try him and see if he works for you.' In that frame of mind, 'choosing Jesus' is not so much a matter of submitting to him in a life-changing act of repentance and commitment, as a matter of opting for the moment to give Jesus a chance to meet my needs – taking him on approval for a free trial with no obligation to buy, as it were. It's a long way from the New Testament, where to accept the declaration 'Jesus is Lord' in the midst of the religious plurality of the Roman empire shut off all other lordship options (1 Cor 8:5-6).

So how then can we think clearly about the uniqueness of Jesus Christ in the midst of the religious supermarket in which we live? What are the different approaches to this question among the specialists? What was, or is, so unique about Jesus anyway? And what does the Bible have to say about the variety of human religions? These are some of the questions we plan to look at in this book.

1

Surveying the Scene

The first thing we need to do is to gain an overview of the complexity of the question we want to think clearly about. This chapter surveys several aspects of religious plurality: its social demands, the problem of multi-faith worship, religious education in schools, popular knowledge about foreign cultures, how people feel about the differences among religions, the myths about Christian missionaries, and the changes in traditional theology. It is important to see that different responses may be needed to each aspect of the problem.

Surveying the Scene

If the differences between the great religions were just a matter of polite discussion among religious people then we might all live more at ease. But they are not, of course. Nor is it only Christians who are concerned about their relationship with other faiths. It is a crucial issue for Muslims, for example, especially for those living in western countries. The chasmic divide between Hinduism and Islam led to the partition of the British Raj into India and Pakistan, while that between Muslims and Orthodox and Catholic Christians is continuing to fragment the Balkan region. Schools struggle with multi-faith education. Churches agonise over multi-faith worship. Local councils battle with linked ethnic and religious community breakdown and violence.

Trying to think clearly in the midst of this mixture of religious, social, cultural and legal factors is made harder by the way all these quite different dimensions of the problem often get confused in popular reactions and prejudices. So it is important to clarify our thinking by sorting out several different aspects of what we mean by religious pluralism.

The social plurality of religions[1]

It is an obvious, observable fact that we in the UK, and in many other western countries also, now live in an irreversibly plural society. People of all the world faiths, whatever their opinions of each other, find themselves living closely together as fellow citizens. This is simply a fact and cannot be argued against, whether we welcome it or resent it. For us in the West this is a fairly recent development. But in some non-western countries, such as India, Christians have lived with social plurality of religions for centuries – and preserved their distinct faith. It is perhaps typical of western blinkers that we tend to imagine that what is a new experience for us is a new phenomenon in the history of Christianity itself.

The result of this social plurality is that Christians in the West are now obliged to come to terms with other faiths – almost as a by-product of citizenship, or at least as a dimension of neighbourliness. You no longer need to be a missionary to meet people of other faiths. In fact, you may well meet more of them, in a more meaningful and long-term framework, by staying at home in some of our cities. The multi-coloured mixture of ethnic communities in Britain is an opportunity and challenge which the Christian community has scarcely accepted yet, let alone responded to adequately.

Living with plurality

All this calls for a social and cross-cultural understanding of other religious communities, for purely human reasons apart from explicitly Christian ones. By that I mean that Christians, who recognise and respect the image of God in all human beings, ought to show a healthy curiosity in everything that makes other people human and to respect their culture, religion and values. This by no means implies agreeing with, or simply 'accepting', anything anybody believes or practises. That is not so much tolerance as mindless apathy (a point we shall return to). But it does mean a deliberate attempt to understand and appreciate others, to avoid prejudices based on ignorance and stereotypes, and to fulfil fundamental biblical obligations towards them as neighbours. Thus, we can welcome informative books such as Christopher Lamb's *Belief in a Mixed Society* (Lion, 1985), for its wealth of detail on the different religious and cultural patterns to be found in the variety of communities in Britain today. Loyalty to Christ should never mean arrogance, superiority or ignorant contempt towards what other people hold precious, even when we disagree with them. Such attitudes are in themselves unChristlike and a denial of the neighbour love he commanded.

Multi-faith worship

How far can we go, however, in the expression of such neighbour love, and does it ever become a compromise of our own commitment to the uniqueness of Christ? Few issues present this problem quite so starkly as the controversy over multi-faith worship. For some, such events are an expression of goodwill and friendship, helping to dissolve prejudices and to promote neighbourly relations. For others they are totally unacceptable because they seem to rest on pluralist assumptions about all religions being equally valid. So they are thus reckoned to amount to a denial of the uniqueness of Christ and the sacredness of his name as the only valid means of approach to God. Sometimes 'thinking clearly' and doing the right thing is very difficult. Put yourself in the following situation:

> You are the vicar of an Anglican parish church with strong civic links in a city with two large minority communities, Hindu and Sikh. In a motorway disaster, several coaches are involved in a horrific crash, and many people in the community have been killed or injured. These include significant numbers from the minority religious communities. The city council proposes to hold a religious service which will give expression to the community's grief, and will honour and commemorate the dead. They write to you requesting the use of the parish church as the venue for the event and invite you to liaise with the religious leaders of the minority communities in preparing the 'programme'. You call a Parish Church Council meeting to discuss the matter before replying to the city council. What will you say to your church council? What decision do you hope they will take, and for what reasons? How will you reply to the city council?

No other name

You might approach the question with the distinction between the different religions in the community uppermost in your mind, and find yourself totally opposed to any use of a building dedicated to the worship of God through Christ for worship involving any other names. There is no shortage of biblical support for this position and it would not be difficult to build your case, even though it will of course be difficult to present it to the city council.

On the other hand, you might approach the question not so much through the category of 'other religions' as through the fundamental biblical teaching on the value of all human beings to God and the demands of being neighbour to those in special need. You might turn to Old Testament texts about care for the alien, and New Testament texts like the parable of the Good Samaritan, and consider the pastoral and social needs of the stricken community more important at this moment than their religious affiliation. Would you agree to let the social plurality of the community, and its need in times of community grief, take priority – in such circumstances – over 'taking a stand for the truth'? How would you weigh up the danger, on the one hand, of compromising the uniqueness of Christ if you agree to the request, with the danger, on the other hand, of being thought to deny the love of Christ if you refuse it?

Do your homework

If you do decide to plan a joint event, or indeed to share in one organised by one of the other religious leaders, you will need to be aware of the differences between Hindu and Sikh concepts of deity also. They may both be 'Indian religions', but they are enormously different. How much homework will you need to do in order to 'think clearly' about how each religious tradition thinks of death and what lies beyond it, of God, or gods, or the transcendent realm, in order to understand and explain the biblical Christian view of these matters in such a context?

These are the kinds of questions that people living in the midst of multi-faith communities face all the time – even if not often in such tragic circumstances. Social and religious plurality forces us to think – which is not a bad thing.

Religion and education

Put yourself in the following situation:

> You are one of the parent-governors at a school where you have a teenage daughter. As part of the Religious Education programme, the children have been taken on several occasions to visit places of worship of other faiths – a Muslim mosque, a Hindu temple, a Jewish synagogue, a Sikh gurudwara. This is followed by discussion and writing up of projects. The RE teacher next proposes that the class prepares to 'experience' the worship of other faiths, by setting up the classroom as an imitation temple, synagogue etc., and making use of the music and prayers and other rituals of different faiths, as far as is practicable. The goal is understanding through involvement. One or two other Christian parents contact you, expressing their unhappiness and saying that this is 'going a bit too far'. What is your response?

Let's sample the varieties of worship

For years now the school of the 'phenomenology of religion', especially as promoted by Ninian Smart, has had a strong influence on Religious Education in British schools. This goes beyond simply the comparative study of the *history and beliefs* of the different religions – which is, of course, a valid and proper educational objective. This approach advocates actual experimentation in the *worship and rituals* of other faiths. Superficially this sounds good in theory as an educational aid. But, as one hears it reported by some teachers, it can amount in practice to a trifling with religion, in a fashion only conceivable in the 'post-religious' cynicism of the West. Christian RE teachers known to me speak of the dominant, assumed pluralism of the staffroom: colleagues there regard it as obvious and to be taken for granted that all religions lead to God anyway (or their followers imagine that they do, if one is an atheist), so why not sample bits of all of them and broaden the children's minds?

Religious rites and practices in all faiths, however, are only the tip of the iceberg. They give outward expression to a whole underlying mass of deep spiritual assumptions and perceptions of reality. They draw their meaning from the world-view within which they are practised. An outsider to the religion needs long exposure to, and genuine interest in, those presuppositions and beliefs before the worship and rituals can be truly appreciated or even understood. It isn't something that can be meaningfully reconstructed on a Thursday afternoon in a crowded curriculum between lunch and hockey. There is the danger of seriously distorting what is supposed to be under study through 'pretend' worship. Worship means vastly different things in different religious world-views, even when rites and customs appear to have similarities. There is also the danger of trivialising something very important. It will not only be Christian parents who may be unhappy about children sharing in the religious actions of others. Small doses of the rituals of other faiths, entered into by school children whose minds are already conditioned by the secular cynicism about religion in general, can have the effect of making the religions themselves seem equally meaningless at best, ridiculous at worst.

The situation is made worse by the exclusion of any critical evaluation of religions in the context of religious education. Not only does our relativistic culture disapprove of such critique, but also our educational philosophy relegates religion to the category of opinion, not of truth. So any evaluation of the truth or falsehood of the tenets of the world's religions will be excluded from the RE classroom. It's a kind of 'look but don't touch' exposure to religions.

Evaluation is necessary

So a generation has emerged from our education system which has rightly shed the former falsehood that Christianity was the white man's religion and therefore was the superior religion just as he belonged to the superior race, but has received in its place only a new falsehood that all religions are as good as each other and equally true (or false, or irrelevant).

Growth in knowledge about other religions

It is certainly true that much more knowledge about the world's religions is available to ordinary people than ever before. Early works on the subject of 'comparative religion' were often a mixture of travellers' tales combined with a large dose of academic theory about the 'obvious' evolution of religion from primitive animism to ethical monotheism, along a straight line of historical progress. Such theorising now seems acutely quaint when read in the light of the great expansion of well-researched information from anthropologists and other first-hand sources. And to this we have to add the extensive articulation of their own beliefs by representatives of the other faiths. You can get teaching at popular level at mosques and temples and synagogues, or you can do degrees to the highest level in the religious departments of universities, taught by the finest intellects of other faiths. So we can now know other faiths in much greater depth than was possible generations ago.

Alongside this scholarly advance, there is also a rising popular interest in other cultures for their own sake. 'Coffee table books' on a wide range of human cultures and curiosities are popular. TV programmes include not only documentaries on other lands and peoples, but holiday guides which increasingly include tourist advice for countries previously considered exotic and inaccessible for tourists such as India, Gambia, North Africa, etc. Such programmes often comment on how to observe and appreciate the religious aspects of the culture one briefly encounters. Films such as *Gandhi* catch people's imagination and certainly challenge our religious assumptions. Even the televising of a major event such as the funeral and cremation of Mrs Indira Gandhi in 1984 brought some of the realities and rites of Hinduism into people's living rooms. So with all this increasing scholarly knowledge and popular awareness of other faiths and cultures, some people are inclined to ask, in all sincerity, 'What is so special about Christianity after all?'

It's all relative

This question becomes the centre of a view called relativism. Relativism is the idea that there are no absolutes, no fixed points, no objective truth. All we have are our own perspectives, or our own social constructions, which are nothing more than that – our own. Since other people and other cultures see things differently, everything is relative. Everybody can be at least partly right. Nobody can say other points of view

No absolutes

are wrong. Relativism is a common philosophy in moral matters these days. Morality, we are told, is all a matter of culture, context, and history. It has no definite or permanent form or standards which are objectively true for all people at all times. There is no transcendent moral God to make moral values fixed and universal. The same goes for religions. Since we now know so much about other cultures than our own, and since we now recognise that all cultures are shaped by history and are constantly changing, we can no longer accept any claim to finality or absoluteness – in anything at all, and certainly not in religion. To the relativist mind, historic Christianity is intolerable because it appears intolerant and absolute, doggedly claiming actually to be true and stubbornly refusing to accept an imposed relativity with good grace. Alan Race, for example, who advocates religious pluralism, commenting on the cultural and historical relativity of all knowledge and all religions, has this to say:

> Given these kinds of assumptions about historically conditioned knowledge, no faith which proclaims itself as absolutely *a priori* the true way can escape the charge of religious arrogance and imperialism.[2]

The trouble is that it is not Christianity as a religion which proclaims itself the only true way, but Jesus himself (as we shall explore in Chapter 4). So are we to accuse Jesus of being a religiously arrogant imperialist? Either we must do so, or else we must assume that the New Testament is mistaken in its portrayal of Jesus. We can choose to recreate our own picture of Jesus to fit our more congenial relativism – and throw away our New Testaments. Or we can take the New Testament witness seriously, in which case Jesus cuts right across that kind of relativism with his astonishing claims.

We shall come back to the matter of relativism and Jesus later, but at this point we can make a small initial response. We can relativise the relativisers! How do they know that everything is relative and there is no absolute or final truth? For if that were true, then even the statement itself 'there is no absolute truth' becomes relative and open to change and challenge. You can't be absolutely relative! Relativism logically destroys itself.

Moral and emotional reactions

These are not always the same thing, of course! But in this particular debate they do tend to get mixed up. If people find something emotionally disturbing, they may see it as also morally unacceptable. And certainly religion raises people's emotional temperature and touches their moral sensibility. When Christians put forward the biblical claim that the God who created the universe has acted for the salvation of humanity only in the biblical history of Israel with its climax in Jesus of Nazareth, and that Jesus is therefore the only way of salvation, there are many who find this offensive. Most often it is accused of being arrogantly dismissive of other great religious figures in history. Some find it immoral that one nation, culture and history should be thus privileged, and unfair that only those who believe in Christ can be saved. God should have been more democratic. What for us as Christians may be a song, for example, of ecstatic devotion to Christ and what he alone has done or can do, may for others sound like immoral exclusivism and arrogance, quite unacceptable in its implications, if not in its sentiments.

W Cantwell Smith argues strongly that any kind of Christian exclusivism is 'morally unacceptable' if it means 'we are saved, you are damned'. He rejects any exclusivist Christology (Jesus is the *only* incarnation of God, or the *only* Saviour) as actually a violation of Christian charity. So he calls on Christians, in the name of Christianity itself, to 'a certain theological surrender' of claims to uniqueness, or even that Jesus is superior or that he is the standard by which other religions must be judged. Similarly, Arnold Toynbee argued that all religions share a common essence and differ only over peripherals. Then he urged that the 'peripheral' which Christianity must be prepared to sacrifice is its claim to uniqueness and superiority. This, he said, was a form of self-centredness which was as immoral for a religion as it is for an individual. This claim to uniqueness, he said, actually contradicts Christianity's own true essence, and should therefore be rejected in order to enable Christianity to realise its essential oneness with other faiths.

Truth sometimes hurts or offends

In response to this kind of objection it can be said that there are many things we would all *like* to believe that are not necessarily true. As human beings our emotions and our moral judgement are both affected by sin so we cannot be sure that how we feel about something is an accurate measure of how true or untrue it is. That is why Christians affirm that it is God's revelation of the truth in the Scriptures and in Christ which is our criterion and authority. And it is often the case that what God says through both cuts across what we would naturally like to hear.

There were things that Jesus said and did that were emotionally

Jesus offended people

upsetting to the disciples, such as giving priority to women, children and the sick, contradicting their ambitions for status by his teaching on servanthood, insisting that he himself was going to suffer and die, washing their feet. If Jesus had allowed himself to be governed as to his message or his mission by the emotional reactions of his contemporaries, he would never have left home, let alone go to the cross. Some of his actions were also regarded as immoral within the understanding of his contemporaries, such as deliberate healing on the Sabbath, mixing with prostitutes, national traitors (Jewish tax-collectors with Rome) and others who scandalised the 'righteous', and making threats against the Temple. If Jesus had stayed within the bounds of what was morally acceptable to people around him, they would never have crucified him.

Paul also discovered that the gospel itself was offensive to certain minds, especially those with the highest religious sensibilities (Jews) and those with the highest philosophical interests (Greeks). A messiah who got crucified as a criminal? Theologically impossible! A God who not only allowed it to happen, but intended it that way? Emotionally repulsive! Bodily resurrection? Philosophically ridiculous! Paul also found that his message that we are put right with God by God's own grace through faith, and not on the basis of our own good works, was opposed by some on moral grounds. They protested that such a belief would open the door to unrestrained sin because people would have no respect for God's law and think God would 'just forgive' them no matter what. Yet if Paul had agreed to a 'theological surrender' of these 'offensive' aspects of Christian faith, he would have abandoned the truth of the gospel altogether. We can be very glad that he didn't. On the contrary, in defending what other people objected to, he wrote most of the letters in our New Testament! Paul's refusal to surrender these key points of the gospel in the face of emotional and moral objections, should at least make us wary of too easily bowing to the same kind of pressure today over the uniqueness or finality of Jesus Christ.

Attitudes to Christian mission

Undoubtedly Christian missions and missionaries are much maligned and misunderstood in the modern world. They can be caricatured as arrogant, and stigmatised as the destroyers of culture. Certainly, they are intolerable to the pluralist mindset. Put yourself in yet another situation.

You are chairperson of the mission committee of your local church. As part of its programme you are hosting a special 'Mission Education' weekend, with Bible studies, workshops on current trends in mission, guest speakers, etc. All goes well, until the meeting when a young missionary couple, who have gone from the church to work in partnership with a diocese in an African country, are reporting on their first term of service. They have been involved in a combination of teaching and administration in a diocese that is seeing rapid church growth and have had some part in training of evangelists and in discipleship courses for new Christians. They are enthusiastic about what they have been involved in and use traditional language about people being converted, coming to faith in Jesus, turning from idolatry, finding salvation in Christ, etc.

After their report, a man stands up who is a lecturer in Religious Studies at the nearby university. Politely at first, but with increasing emotional vigour, he expresses amazement that missionary work should be regarded as acceptable today. 'Have we not left the colonial days behind and come to recognise the value and legitimacy of all cultures?' he asks. 'What gives us the right to denigrate other people's religion as "idolatry" and call them to abandon it for our western religion? How can we go on thinking that Christianity is the only true religion when theologians have been saying for years that biblical language about Jesus as "Lord" and "God" and "Saviour" is not literally true, but rather the expression of love and devotion. While we may have found in Jesus an acceptable symbol for our own search for the ultimate truth, we cannot impose him on others who have their own paths and religious leaders.'

The young couple make a polite and humble reply, pointing out that they are not themselves doing evangelism, but providing support for the African church's own energetic efforts, so it isn't just western colonialism. But in order to dissipate the embarrassment, you offer to meet the objector and discuss the issue after the meeting. What are your thoughts during the final hymn?!

The colonial myth

The lecturer's remarks reveal common enough misunderstandings about mission, as well as indicating the kind of theological stance he takes. We'll look at the theological point in the next section. The couple answered the first misunderstanding by pointing out that they were not western evangelists converting pagan foreigners from a position of colonial superiority, but were merely participating in the confident evangelism of the post-colonial African church itself (which would have gone on without them!). The idea that mission means colonial arrogance is not only a tired myth (i.e., it was never wholly true even in colonial days), but is actually an insult to the vigorous and wholly indigenous mission of the majority church of the Two-Thirds World. Recently I heard an African Christian leader say that it is time that western
Not a Christians realised that the African church is already post
western post-colonial! The fact of the matter is that Christianity is
religion not 'the western religion' any more. It wasn't western in its
origins either, of course, even if the conversion of Europe did lead to centuries when Christianity was predominantly linked with the dominance of European power and culture. But the simple fact is that more than 75% of all the world's Christians now live in the non-western countries of the South and East and by AD

2010, on present trends, most Christian mission will be coming from those countries as well. It is simply nonsense to say that belief in the uniqueness of Christ and the truth of the Christian faith is dependent on the imperialist superiority of 'Christian' nations. These beliefs are held and lived out by millions of Christians in thousands of cultures, many of them poor and oppressed. Some clear thinking is needed on this point as well!

Theological changes

Over the last few decades there has been a trend among some theologians to popularise a new way of talking about Christ. The idea is to reinterpret the traditional Christian language in a way which is not an embarrassment in this modern scientific age. Sometimes the new language is as bewildering to ordinary people as the old was said to be. However, we must take a brief look at it because it eventually 'filters through' to ordinary Christians and certainly affects how people think about Christianity and other religions. It will mean tackling one or two technical words which I hope I can explain well enough to keep us thinking clearly.

Will the **really** real Jesus please stand up

The church's foundational resource for understanding the identity and significance of Jesus is of course the New Testament and its Old Testament roots. Then came the classic historical definitions of his nature in the great creeds of the early centuries. In the face of conflicting views over the nature of Christ, the church councils produced statements like the Nicene creed and the definition of Chalcedon. Now the language of the creeds is (here it comes) *ontological*. Ontology (a Greek word, as you might expect!) means talking about what is real, what something truly is in itself, the nature of things as they really are; *What Jesus* it refers to essential being, not external qualities. *was*

Ontological statements about Christ, then, are ones which talk about his being and nature – what he really was and is in himself, as distinct from statements which tell us what he was like (descriptive statements) or what he did or does (functional statements).

In the New Testament, ontological statements about Jesus would include the opening words of John's Gospel, 'In the beginning was the Word, and the Word was with God, and the Word was God,' or the opening line of an early Christian hymn, 'Christ Jesus, being in very nature God...' (Phil 2:6), or Paul's affirmation, 'He [Christ] is the image of the invisible God, the firstborn over all creation' (Col 1:15). In the creeds, ontological statements include, for example, the affirmation that he is 'God from God, light from light, very God of very God, one in being with the Father ...' Essentially, the New Testament, the creeds and the church's historic Christology ('Christology' means teaching about Jesus Christ) all affirm that Jesus Christ, in the fullest sense of his being, was and is both fully human and fully God.

Love language

Now, the reinterpreters ask us to regard all such language as 'confessional language' – an outpouring of love and faith towards Jesus for what he has done for us, but expressed in terms which seem to describe what he is. We should not take the ontological statements as literally true, but rather regard them as functionally significant. The statement 'My Lord and my God' on the lips of Thomas means only 'In Jesus I have found what God can mean to me,' not 'Jesus actually is Lord and God.' It is love language, not objective truth. So then, the case goes on, if we want to retain the uniqueness of Jesus, we must recognise that Jesus is unique only in terms of what God has done through him as a very special person, or because of what he showed us about God through his amazingly close relationship with God, not because he himself was actually divine. The emphasis is, 'Jesus was unique in the *degree* to which, as a human being, he had a relationship with God,' rather than 'Jesus was unique in *kind,* as the one and only incarnation of God in a fully human person and life.'

Myth

The doctrine of the incarnation (the affirmation that God became truly and fully human in the birth and life of Jesus of Nazareth), is to be understood as a *myth*. Scholars who propose this are using the term 'myth' in a special way which is different from its use in common language of some legend or idea which everybody realises to be false or exaggerated. Scholars use 'myth' to mean a story which, while not literally true in itself (it may not have happened at all, or it may have happened but not in the way the story records), nevertheless gives expression to some truth of life or experience. A myth may therefore be not true at the level of historical fact, but profoundly true in what it expresses about human life in the world. Or a myth may be a story told to explain or justify the way the *Myth-Christology* world is, or how things got to be the way they are. The 'myth of God incarnate', according to this view, was a story by which those who experienced Jesus gave expression to what they saw of God in Jesus. But for us, with our modern scientific and historical knowledge, it cannot be accepted as a statement of fact. Jesus was certainly very special, but he was not more than human. And so, concludes Alan Race, 'viewing Jesus in this way, [i.e. only in terms of God's action through him as a man, not as himself divine]... rescues Christianity from embarrassment in an age of radical historical consciousness.'[3]

Now this has generated a lot of debate in the church, which is far beyond the scope of this book to survey.[4] But as regards the debate we are concerned with here over religious pluralism, you will find that those who adopt a pluralist approach to other faiths are very keen on this 'myth-Christology', as a way of re-interpreting what the New Testament says about Jesus. It fits perfectly. Indeed it seems to me that it is impossible to move to a theologically pluralist position and still claim allegiance to the New Testament unless you make some such reinterpretation of the New Testament witness.[5] We shall return to this question more fully in our critique of pluralism in Chapter 4.

Mind the gaps!

Religious plurality, then, is a social fact. In trying to think clearly about it as Christians we need to make careful distinctions about its different dimensions. We need to look at the context in which particular issues arise and not assume that every instance involving people of other faiths is implicitly an attack upon the uniqueness of Jesus Christ. We might accept something in the context of an educational programme that we would not accept in explicit acts of worship. We might accept something in a civic building that we would not accept in a Christian church. We might do something in a personal, private and pastoral context (e.g. praying with a Muslim in her own home) that we would decline to do in a public context where different assumptions would be made and implications drawn.

It is also important to avoid mixing up responses to one dimension of the problem with responses to others. For example, the fact of the *social* plurality of different religious communities does not change *theological* truths. By that I mean that the truth or falsehood of a particular Christian teaching does not depend on sociological changes. Changes in society, culture, population, etc. certainly do mean that Christians constantly have to rethink and re-express their beliefs. This has always been true, and in a sense all Christian theology is an attempt to express the faith in such a way that its truth addresses and is understood within new social and cultural contexts. Since Christians in the West are now much more closely in contact with people of other faiths, they are indeed called on to examine and explain what traditional Christian credal statements mean by saying that Jesus is the unique incarnation of God. But either he is and always has been uniquely God, or he is not and never has been. The truth of the matter is not affected by the changing shape and religious texture of society.

And if social plurality rightly makes us feel the necessity of expressing love and understanding to the people in different religious communities, that does not simply dissolve the theological distinctions and conceptual conflicts that exist between the Christian faith and other beliefs. People easily slip from a right desire to be nice to others into the idea that it is therefore wrong to hold on to beliefs that contradict other people's religion. We confuse tolerance for people we disagree with, with tolerance of their ideas themselves, which is very different. It used to be quite accepted that we could say to others, 'I utterly disagree with your beliefs, but I respect and care for you as a person and will treat you accordingly.' Now however we are pressurised into feeling that to regard anyone else's beliefs as wrong is to victimise them. It is not 'politically correct'. It is branded intolerant. But to affirm (biblically) that all human beings are equal and valuable is not to say that anything human beings believe is equally true and valid. Social tolerance does not mean agreeing that everybody is right!

Charity and clarity

But there are dangers to avoid in the opposite direction also. We may have a *theological* commitment of exclusive loyalty to Jesus Christ as the only true incarnation of God and the only Saviour of human beings, but that does not justify *social* attitudes of exclusivism, bigotry or rejection. Christians have sadly often fallen into this danger. In fact the history of the church is full of the horrors that come from turning exclusive understandings of the gospel into sectarian social attitudes and matching action – crusades and pogroms being the worst examples. Believing that others are religiously wrong does not mean rejecting or hating them as human persons! We need charity as well as clarity; to love dearly as well as to think clearly.

2

Jesus Exclusively at the Centre

In the previous chapter we made a number of clarifications and distinctions which should help us take a more thoughtful and sensitive approach to those of other faiths in our midst and in other lands. In this chapter we shall begin a survey of three main positions that have been adopted by Christian theologians towards other religions: exclusivism, inclusivism and pluralism. First comes exclusivism and we shall carefully define what it does, and does not, mean. But even those who are firmly convinced that salvation is exclusively to be found in Jesus Christ differ over the question as to what will happen to those who never hear of Christ in their lifetime. We shall look at three ways of answering that question.

Jesus Exclusively at the Centre

It has become quite common in this debate to adopt this broad classification of the different Christian approaches to other faiths into three main views: *exclusivism, inclusivism* and *pluralism.* Obviously things are never as simple as a threefold classification, but some simplification is welcome in a debate as complex as this! So let us make use of these three terms as a framework for this and the next two chapters.[1] It might be helpful to begin with a concise definition of each position, as provided by Harold Netland:

> *Exclusivism* maintains that the central claims of Christianity are true, and that where the claims of Christianity conflict with those of other religions, the latter are to be rejected as false. Christian exclusivists also characteristically hold that God has revealed himself definitively in the Bible and that Jesus Christ is the unique incarnation of God, the only Lord and Saviour. Salvation is not to be found in the structures of other religious traditions.
>
> *Inclusivism,* like exclusivism, maintains that the central claims of the Christian faith are true, but it adopts a much more positive view of other religions than does exclusivism. Although inclusivists hold that God has revealed himself definitively in Jesus Christ and that Jesus is somehow central to God's provision of salvation for humankind, they are willing to allow that God's salvation is available through non-Christian religions. Jesus is still held to be, in some

sense, unique, normative, and definitive; but God is said to be revealing himself and providing salvation through other religious traditions as well. It is the attempt to strike the delicate balance between the affirmation of God's unique revelation and salvation in Jesus Christ and openness to God's saving activity in other religions that distinguishes inclusivism.

Pluralism parts company with both exclusivism and inclusivism by rejecting the premise that God has revealed himself in any unique or definitive sense in Jesus Christ. To the contrary, God is said to be actively revealing himself in all religious traditions. Nor is there anything unique or normative about the person of Jesus. He is simply one of many great religious leaders who have been used by God to provide salvation for humankind. Pluralism, then, goes beyond inclusivism in rejecting the idea that there is anything superior, normative, or definitive about Chrisitianity. Christian faith is merely one of many equally legitimate human responses to the same divine reality.[2]

What exclusivism does not mean

We must first of all make clear what exclusivism does not, or should not, mean. The word is *not* being used in a personal, attitudinal or social sense, i.e. pride, superiority and a desire to exclude others. Rather the word is being used here in the theological sense. That is, it is not talking about exclusive people, but about exclusive truth. It is concerned only with the matter of where truth and salvation are to be found. It is the view that, if Jesus Christ be uniquely the truth, and the only way of salvation for mankind, then that *excludes* the possibility of other faiths being true in the same way, or being ways of salvation. Used in this way, any human statement that claims to be true, or is accepted by everybody as true, is necessarily exclusive of other statements which contradict or deny it. If I tell you that my name is Chris Wright, and that is accepted as true, then it excludes the possibility that I am Charles Wilkinson. If we agree on the truth of the statement that Paris is the capital of France, we exclude the proposition that Lyons is the capital of France. The truth that two and two make four excludes the possibility that in some circumstances they might make five.[3]

Exclusive truth

So, in matters of truth, exclusivism is not a negative attitude, but a simple necessity of human thought and speech.[4]

What exclusivism maintains

The main features of this position may be outlined as follows:

– There is one living, personal God who is the Creator of all that is, including ourselves. As human beings, uniquely of all creatures, we are made in God's image and are spiritually aware of God and morally accountable to God.

– Human beings have rebelled against God in the moral disobedience of sin, and are alienated from God in such a radical way that they cannot save themselves or know God truly by themselves.

– God has taken action to reveal himself and to save human beings uniquely through the history of Old Testament Israel since Abraham, with the intention of bringing blessing to all nations.

– Jesus of Nazareth was the unique and final incarnation of God in a single historical human life. He both completed God's self-revelation, and achieved God's work of salvation on the cross. Through his resurrection and ascension God vindicated him as Lord and so he is rightly to be worshipped as such.

– Salvation is therefore to be found only in and through Jesus Christ. Adherents of other faiths, in common with all human beings, are made in the image of God and share in the benefits of general revelation in conscience and nature. But other faiths as such cannot be ways of salvation, for that is only in Christ.

– There is therefore a radical discontinuity between the revelation and salvation of God in Christ and other religions.[5]

Exclusivism is usually associated with the conservative evangelical position. But the major champion of this view in the twentieth century was unquestionably the great Swiss theologian Karl Barth. Writing in reaction to early twentieth century liberalism, he produced a massive defence of divine revelation as over against all human religion, and an assertion of the sovereign freedom of God. God, he argued, can be encountered only in Christ, and all other religions which are not based on Christ are therefore unbelief by definition and assumption. Even Christianity, as a human religion, he argued, can be a form of unbelief at any point where it fails to live solely by the grace of Christ.[6]

The critics

The exclusivist position draws a lot of criticism, both from the secular world (where the supermarket mentality reigns), and from some Christian theologians who regard it as an impossibly narrow understanding of the Christian faith. Even critics who reject this view of other faiths, however, admit that exclusivism (in its theological definition, as sketched above) is a very strong position, biblically, logically and historically. Alan Race, for example, though totally opposed to such a view himself, says of exclusivism:

> It appeals to what for many is a self-evident biblical witness; it gives a central function to the person of Christ; the internal logic of the argument appears consistent and coherent; and, finally, it is the position which corresponds most closely to what has generally been held to be orthodox Christianity through the centuries.[7]

Thus Race says that he finds it difficult to criticise, though it is a difficulty he quickly overcomes. First he asks if it is an appropriate response to the new knowledge we now have about the world religions. But, while it is certainly true, as we said in Chapter 1, that increasing understanding of other faiths must affect our attitude to those who follow them, it does not in itself affect the truth or falsehood of either their beliefs or ours. This objection of Race is also somewhat affected by western blinkers. The 'new knowledge' we have about other religions may be new to western Christians, but has been a fact of life for other Christians who, while living in the midst of those religions for centuries, have not felt it necessary to reject the central and exclusive claims of the Christian faith.

Then Race also adds that we cannot condemn the majority of humanity to hell on the force of logic. No indeed, but then it is not we who condemn anyone to hell. Such judgements lie in the just and merciful hand of Almighty God. The question is, do we have any criteria on which that judgement will be made, so that it can be avoided? And if the exclusivist position attempts to chalk out criteria which are biblically grounded and logically consistent, it needs to be answered on those grounds, for we will certainly not get humanity into heaven on the force of illogic either.

How exclusive can you get?

When we examine the views of evangelicals, however, who are most usually identified with the exclusivist view, we find considerable difference of opinion on the degree of exclusivism adopted. This is especially so over the issue of the extent of salvation. While there would be agreement among evangelical Christians that 'salvation is through Jesus Christ alone' (indeed that is one of the defining core elements of evangelical identity), the question asked is, does that necessarily mean 'salvation is only through actual knowledge of Jesus Christ and conscious faith in him'? Or to put the matter another way: it is accepted on all sides among evangelicals that whoever will finally be saved and join the redeemed people of God in the new creation will be so on the sole basis of the cross of Christ. All salvation is because of what God has done in and through Jesus Christ, his incarnate Son. There is no other source or means of salvation. But is it possible for anyone to be saved who has not heard of Christ and thus cannot explicitly trust in him? The question is sometimes framed in theological language. We affirm the *ontological* necessity of Christ for salvation (salvation is through the *fact* of the cross and resurrection of Christ and there is no other means of salvation for anybody). But this can be distinguished from the *epistemological* necessity of Christ for salvation (salvation is through the *knowledge* of the gospel and you have to *know* about Christ in order to be saved by him). All evangelicals would affirm the first. Some would insist on the second also, but others would not.

We must think clearly about the question itself before trying to answer it. It is not asking if people can be saved by some other way than by Christ, such as by another religion; that is not at issue, because it is granted that there is no salvation outside the work of Christ. Also, the question is not asking whether people who reject Christ might nevertheless possibly be saved, but refers only to those who have had no opportunity in their lifetime to hear about him and make any kind of choice regarding him – those who have never heard the gospel, the unevangelised. Is there any possibility that God saves any such people through Christ even though they have not heard of him? That is the question.

There are broadly three ways in which the question is answered among evangelical Christians today:

i) *'Definitely no'*. All human beings stand under the just judgement of God for their sin and rebellion. The only way of salvation is through repentance and faith in the saving work of Christ on the cross. Therefore, those who never hear of Jesus in their life on this earth are eternally lost. Biblical support for such a view of the matter is strong and clearly laid out by those who affirm it. They point to texts such as Matthew 7:13-14; John 14:6; Acts 4:12; Romans 10:13-14; 1 John 5:12. This view clearly defines and defends the uniqueness of Christ in unequivocal terms. Not only is Christ the only means of salvation available to humanity, but also hearing and responding to the gospel of Christ is the only means by which the salvation achieved by Christ can be received. This is sometimes supported by the argument that, if this were not so, what motive would be left for evangelism?[8]

This position has been termed 'restrictivism' by John Sanders[9] – i.e. it is that form of the exclusivist view that affirms that salvation will finally be restricted to those who hear the gospel and believe in Jesus. The term 'restrictivism' suffers from the same aura of negativity that the word exclusivism itself does, but it can be defended in the same way as we did for exclusivism – namely that it is talking about a restricted *category* as a matter of truth or fact, not about a restrictive *attitude* or bigotry as a personal characteristic. It is still difficult, however, to disassociate the term, or the teaching it represents, from negative overtones that easily lead to misrepresentation and distortion of what it stands for.

'Through no fault of their own?'

One particular distortion of this view needs to be tackled immediately since it is so commonly put forward. 'How can you believe that God will condemn people to hell *just because* they have not believed in Jesus, if they have never heard of him? It is not their fault that they have not heard of Jesus, since they have never been evangelised, so it is manifestly unfair to condemn them for not responding to the gospel.' This can be made to sound so plausible that it is especially important to think clearly at this point. The Bible never teaches or even hints that God's judgement is aimed at people because they have not responded to the Christ of whom they have never heard. What it does unquestionably and uncompromisingly teach is that all human beings are sinful and stand rightly under God's judgement, whether they *The reason* have heard of Christ or not. Of course the Bible also *for God's* shows clearly that not everybody is as wicked as *judgement* everybody else; and that not everybody is as wicked as they could be. But it leaves us in no doubt of the fundamental and universal fact of human sinfulness and wickedness. And it is *that* which is the reason for God's judgement. Those who will finally experience the wrath of God and all that is intended by the Bible's warnings about hell will do so, not because of what they did not know and could not do (i.e. trust in Jesus), but because of all they did know and nevertheless did (i.e. sin against the light of conscience and the knowledge of God available to all, cf. Rom 1:18-32). To put it more bluntly and simply: nobody will go to hell *because* they never heard of Jesus. If the suggestion that they might seems impossibly unfair to us, then how much less do we imagine God could operate in such a way, when the Bible affirms that, as Judge of all the earth, he will do what is absolutely right.

Guilty sinner or innocent victim?

But we need to be careful when bringing the idea of 'fairness' in here. One of the characteristics of human sin is that we very readily jump to accuse others (including God) for being unfair while exonerating ourselves of all blame. This aspect of the stories of Adam and Eve and Cain and Abel is lived out in every childhood and modelled to perfection in many politicians! On this issue, those who reject the exclusivist (restrictivist) position may fall into collusion with this human habit. Whereas the clear thrust of the Bible from cover to cover is on the justice of God and the guilt of human beings, we are invited instead to be shocked at the unfairness of God and the innocence of human beings. God is *Perversion of biblical teaching* to be blamed if anybody is *not* saved, rather than praised and adored because anybody *is* saved. People are unevangelised 'through no fault of their own', it is said, therefore they are sent to hell 'through no fault of their own'. But such language is a perversion of biblical teaching. It will not do, and it certainly is no help to clear thinking, to switch off the biblical spotlight of God's righteous judgement and replace it with a banner proclaiming our unfair victimisation. To repeat: nobody goes to hell *because* they have not heard of Christ, but because of their sin and rebellion in the sight of God – which the Bible affirms is the universal condition of all humanity.[10]

ii) *'Possibly yes'*. There are other evangelical Christians who would just as strongly affirm that the cross of Christ is the only ground for human salvation, but would be less certain that the number of the saved will ultimately be limited to those who hear the gospel and consciously trust in Jesus Christ. They wish to leave open the possibility that God may save through Christ some who, while never having heard of Christ, turn to God in some kind of repentance and faith that only God can evaluate with his intimate knowledge of every human heart. Several arguments are put forward in support of this view.

Old Testament believers

There were believers in the Old Testament whom we would unquestionably regard as 'saved', yet they never knew Jesus of Nazareth. Their salvation was still a matter of God's grace and initiative, and was based on the sacrifice of Christ yet to come in history. That is, they were indeed saved *by* Christ, but not through knowing Christ. Now the force of this line of argument can be reduced by remembering that the people of Israel did have unique revelation of God as Yahweh with all the redemptive and covenantal depths that flowed through their historical experience of God. In theological terms, they had access to more than the general revelation available to all human beings and enjoyed additionally the benefits of special revelation through historical events and prophetic words. Nevertheless the fact is that they did not know of the historical Jesus nor hear 'the gospel' in its New Testament form – i.e. the preaching of the cross of Christ and the necessity of repentance and faith in him. They believed in God in response to what they knew of God through the progress of revelation to that point. And God responded to them in grace and saving righteousness.

Abraham is held as the model of this saving faith, expressed through obedience, in both Testaments. *A model of faith* 'Abraham believed God, and it was credited to him as righteousness' (Gen 15:6 and cf. Rom 4:3). According to Paul, Abraham did respond to the gospel, but not the gospel in its New Testament form as related specifically to Jesus Christ. Rather, he says, 'The Scripture... announced the gospel in advance to Abraham: "All nations will be blessed through you"' (Gal 3:8). The 'good news' in the context of Genesis was that God intended to bless all the nations of humanity in spite of sin and rebellion and to do so by means of the descendants of Abraham.

Non-Israelite believers

But the Old Testament also includes among those to whom God responded graciously others who did not stand within the covenant nation, such as 'converts' like the widow of Zarephath (1 Kings 17:24) and Naaman (2 Kings 5:15-18), repentant sinners such as the Ninevites (Jonah), and some proverbially righteous people like Noah, Job and Daniel (Ezek 14:14, 20). And there were those who were saved who lived long before the redemptive revelation embodied in the history of Israel had even begun, such as Enoch and Noah. Enoch's faith is held up also in the New Testament as a model, and specifically noted as that which is required in order to please God. Hebrews 11:5-6 plainly states that 'Enoch was commended as one who pleased God. And without faith it is impossible to please God, because anyone who comes to him must believe that he exists and that he rewards those who earnestly seek him.' Obviously no mention could be made of faith *in Christ,* since that was impossible for Enoch. However, he certainly trusted God and earnestly sought him. So the question certainly can be asked: if it was possible for people at that time to be saved by Christ without actually knowing Christ because it was *historically* impossible, is it not likewise possible for people today to be saved by Christ even if they do not know him because of geographical and other obstacles? Such people, though living in the 'AD world', are as yet 'informationally BC'. That is to say, in terms of their knowledge, they are in the same position as those who lived before Christ.[11] Are there people like Enoch among them, who believe in God and earnestly seek him? Those who hold this position want to hope so, and to believe that if there are (and only God knows the truth of the matter), then God responds to them in saving grace.

Children dying in infancy and the mentally defective

Another argument sometimes put forward in relation to this view relates to children dying in infancy, and those of such mental deficiency that they cannot understand and respond to the message of the gospel in any articulate way, as far as we can tell. The point is that if such persons are saved (as has been the dominant view of most church traditions down the ages, with some exceptions and qualifications), then they are saved without knowing about Jesus and exercising intelligent faith in him. Again, if this is so, it appears to allow that the number of the finally saved will not be quite identical to the number of those who hear and respond to the gospel. This seems to me a relatively weak argument, both because there is no clear biblical teaching on the matter either way, and also because we can hardly make an exact comparison between the relative moral innocence of infants and the mentally deficient on the one hand and the moral guilt of responsible adult sinners on the other. Nevertheless, it carries some weight if it does nothing more than suggest that more human beings will be saved than those who explicitly and intelligently confess faith in Jesus, and so it leads some to the cautiously hopeful openness of this second view.

If we want to argue along this line we have to be very careful to think clearly about what is *not* being said. First, this is not salvation in the end for everybody, a universalism which believes that everybody will be saved no matter *Caution and clarity* what they believe or how they live. Rather it is saying that there is a basic principle which applies to all human beings, namely that we are saved by God's grace only, received through the channels of repentance and trust in God's mercy. If any human being, realising his or her own inability to live even by the standards of their own conscience, repents of self-effort and failure, and turns to plead the mercy of God, however he or she envisages God, will God not respond in the saving grace of Christ, even if the person never hears of Christ in this life?[12]

Secondly, it is not salvation by sincerity. This view is not saying that good and sincere people in any other faith, or within Christianity either, are saved by their goodness and sincerity. In fact it is the precise opposite of that. In Jesus' shocking parable of the tax-collector and the Pharisee, it was the religious man in his very commendable goodness who was *not* justified, while the sinner who could do nothing but cry for mercy, went home, according to Jesus, 'justified before God' (Lk 18:9-14). All who will be saved in the end will be saved by the grace of God, not because of goodness or merit, and the heart of the gospel is that God saves *sinners* who know they are sinners and turn away from sin and self towards God.

Thirdly, this view is not salvation by other religions, saying that people in other faiths can be saved through the 'sacraments' of their own religious systems, or that other religions are provisional ways of salvation. That is one of the inclusivist viewpoints which we shall look at in the next chapter. The New Testament does not talk of salvation except in and through Christ. In any case, it is God who saves, not religions. It is one thing to say that God may save through the sacrifice of Christ a person who turns to God in repentance within *the context* of another religion; it is quite different to say that that other religion is itself *the means* of the person's salvation. In allowing the possibility of the former, one is not at all affirming the latter. The view we are considering is really a sub-set of the exclusivist position.[13] Salvation is exclusively through Christ and there is no saving dimension to other religions.

iii) *'Definitely yes'*. A third answer to the question moves beyond the caution of the second view. While still affirming with equal strength that Jesus Christ alone is the final revelation of God in history and the sole source of salvation (and thus maintaining an essential pillar of the exclusivist evangelical conviction), those who hold this view are not satisfied with the cautious optimism of the second view (that there are grounds for hoping that God will save some who never hear of Christ, but we cannot ultimately know and must leave the matter in his just and merciful hands), and believe there are biblical grounds for a much more affirmative optimism. This view asserts that there will be multitudes who have never heard of Christ in their earthly lifetime who will nevertheless be among those saved by God's grace and through the saving work of Christ. It has been most strongly put forward recently by Clark Pinnock and John Sanders.[14]

'Pagan saints'

A number of biblical arguments are put forward in support of this position. The existence of believers who were saved in the Old Testament period is given a much greater significance than in the second view above. Pinnock, for example, coins the term 'pagan saints' for those who were not part of the covenant community of Israel and yet exercised faith or became worshippers of Yahweh. But rather than regarding these as exceptional, he regards them more as 'prototypes', or as the tip of the iceberg of a much larger quantity of unknown such people all over the world.

Advocates of this view also suggest that the more traditional Christian viewpoint on this matter has been influenced by taking

A different starting point

as 'control texts' certain passages of the Bible which emphasise God's wrath and judgement, and some which have given rise to the belief that the final number of the saved will be 'few' in relation to the totality of the human race (e.g. Matt 7:13-14; Rom 1-3; Eph 2:12). From that starting point, other texts which affirm the universality of God's saving love (e.g. Jn 12:32; 1 Tim 2:3-6; 4:10; Tit 2:11; 2 Pet 3:9; 1 Jn 2:2), have to be 'explained'. What would be the effect, asks Pinnock, if we were to reverse the direction of our biblical arguing: take the latter kind of text as our starting-point and 'control texts', and then come to the judgement texts in the light of them? The result, he suggests, would be a much greater optimism about salvation without sacrificing either the uniqueness and finality of Christ or the Bible's teaching about the reality of judgement for the wicked and impenitent.[15]

The great final vision of the Bible includes the prospect of a great multitude 'from every nation, tribe, people and language standing before the throne and in front of the Lamb' (Rev 7:9). Unless this is taken in a general and symbolic sense ('from all kinds of peoples'), it may also imply that the final number of the redeemed will include more than those who have been explicitly evangelised since many tribes and peoples and languages have died out in human history long before the gospel reached them (and indeed before Christ was born). So if, on the Last Day, some people will have been saved from those tribes and peoples, they will certainly have been saved by Christ, but without having heard of Christ.

Another argument for this position is known as 'universal accessibility of salvation'. This is not 'universalism' – the view that all human beings will be saved in the end. Rather it is the view that at least the possibility of being saved must be accessible to all human beings. It is not saying that God is under some obligation to save everybody, but rather that if God is truly impartial in his love, then there must be at least an equal opportunity for all to be saved. This is derived from texts which affirm God's desire that all should be saved and that Christ died for all. If such texts are to be meaningful, it is argued, then God must have made it possible in principle and in reality for all to be saved, even though it is accepted that many will not be, because the Bible clearly teaches that there will be people who intentionally remain in their sin and reject God's mercy. It would seem incompatible, however, that God should desire the salvation

Equal opportunity

of all, and yet create people who would live and die without even the possibility of ever being saved at all.[16] Thus both Pinnock and Sanders wish to give much greater priority in the question of the destiny of the unevangelised to the boundless generosity and impartiality of the love and grace of God.

Critics of this position claim that it indulges in exegesis of biblical texts which sometimes does not take proper account of context,[17] and sometimes seems rather forced;[18] that it is unbalanced in its portrayal of the love of God while underplaying God's wrath against the wicked; and that it is too vague in talking about 'faith' without specifying the object of faith – which in New Testaments terms is almost exclusively faith in the person and work of Jesus Christ.[19]

In God's hands

Speaking for myself, I find myself unpersuaded by some of the arguments that advocate position (iii). But I am not as certain as Carson that the case against position (iii) sweeps aside position (ii) as well, leaving us no option but position (i). I find it hard to accept that the sovereign saving grace of God is limited to the evangelistic obedience or effectiveness of the church, and so remain unconvinced that position (i) expresses the total biblical truth on the matter. That is, it seems that a strict adherence to the restrictivist view means that one has to say in effect that God is not able or not willing to save anybody unless and until Christians have reached them with an intelligible preaching of the gospel to which they have properly responded. It is possible, of course, that God may have chosen to set such a limitation on saving grace and we are not in any position to question his sovereign right to do so. However, it does raise the question of apparent fairness in the ways of God again. By that I do *not* mean the charge that it is unfair in itself that some should be saved and some not. That is a distortion which we dealt with above, in which God is quite falsely blamed for the non-salvation of any sinners. No person under the final judgement of God will be able to say 'it's not fair', for God's perfect justice will be recognised and acknowledged. Rather what seems *prima facie* unfair is that the criterion of who may or who may not have the opportunity of being saved at all should depend entirely and exclusively upon the human obedience of the church, and upon its patchy success even when it was trying to be obedient, to say nothing of those periods when it was shamefully marked by virtually zero evangelistic effort. Especially since, by that criterion (and within the foreknowledge of God) many millions of the human race for many centuries have had not the remotest chance of being saved – no one at all, for example, in the American continents until the last quarter of the Christian era, and even then the 'Christianity' with which they were 'evangelised' was scarcely good news for many of them.[20]

Accordingly, I find myself among those in position (ii) who believe that among the finally saved there will be those whom God has saved through Christ who, though not knowing of Jesus, turned in some measure of repentance and faith to God, found grace in the eyes of the Lord, and will meet their Saviour with surprise and joy when he welcomes them to his kingdom. Who, where, when and how many they may be I am content to leave in the hands of God, trusting in the perfect justice and mercy of the God who knows the hearts of all his creatures.[21]

Motivation for evangelism

Let's return finally to a point that was made in support of position (i), namely that unless one accepts the restrictivist view (that those who never hear the gospel are without exception eternally lost), one is left with no motive for evangelism. For those who believe this, even position (ii) is suspected as producing diminished motivation. To this I would make two responses.

First, it is not at all a necessary result that position (ii) removes motivation for evangelism and in fact it simply isn't true in experience for many, including myself. Among those who adopt position (ii) are some, like John Stott, whose commitment to evangelism and their life-long involvement in it are beyond question. The hopeful possibility that God *A matter of* may in his sovereign grace save some whom one can *urgency and* never reach with the gospel does not in any way lessen *obedience* the church's obligation in mission and evangelism. We know that the human race universally lives in a state of sin and under God's judgement; that God has provided the means of salvation in the cross and resurrection of Christ; and that we are commanded by Christ himself to make these facts known to the nations and to call all men and women to respond to them in repentance, faith and obedience. We have no liberty to preach otherwise, if we are to be obedient to this commission. If, however, God in the sovereignty of his grace, but independently of human evangelistic activity, initiates in the heart of any human being a response of repentance and faith which leads to their final salvation through Christ, then this will by definition be unknown to us and known only to God. It will be a matter of rejoicing and giving greater glory to God, but it gives us no more valid reason to disobey the Great Commission than does the biblical doctrine of election, though that too has been accused of being a disincentive to evangelism.

Second, we need to think more clearly about the motivation itself. There is no doubt that the belief that those who never hear of Jesus are inevitably lost has been one of the major motives in

What kind of motive? the modern missionary movement, though certainly not the only one. And, of course, it also does reflect the biblical teaching about the awfulness of human sin and the righteousness and finality of God's judgement. But the question here is not whether the perilous state of all human beings apart from the saving light of the gospel is a motive to engage in evangelism. Of course it is. The question is whether it is the case that if one allows that God may save any at all apart from the explicit hearing of the gospel, then one is left with no motive to evangelise. I do not accept that this is so.

We also need to distinguish between motivation which is *effective* and that which is also *true*. A good and positive goal may be motivated by arguments which are effective, but not necessarily the truth, or the whole truth. For example, parents may try to make children behave well with the threat that otherwise Santa Claus will not bring presents. The motive may be effective (i.e. successful in getting the children to be good), but it is not based on truth. However, to recognise the falsehood inherent in the motivation does not mean that children should no longer behave well! Or again, imagine that new drivers could all be persuaded that if they drive faster than 50mph the wheels of the car will fall off. It would be effective motivation for safe driving, but not true. To realise it was not true would, again, not mean that we no longer need to drive safely. Similarly, to believe that all who never hear the gospel are inevitably and without exception eternally lost is certainly effective motivation for evangelism (i.e. it has historically been successful in getting many people burdened to evangelise with great zeal). But even if it is not wholly true, or is an exaggeration of the final truth, and if one is convinced that a biblical case can be made that God will save some who do not know Christ in their lifetime, that does not reduce the importance or the centrality of evangelism as a primary duty of the church. For in the end the only way *we* can be sure that people are being saved is as we are faithful in our witness and see people responding in repentance and faith to Christ. That is our task, our duty and our joy. Beyond that, let God be God.

A primary duty of the church

3

Jesus Inclusively at the Centre

Having explored the exclusivist position we turn now to the second dominant way of viewing world religions from a Christian angle – inclusivism. As before we shall try to define the term clearly and then look at two main varieties of it, with special attention to the Roman Catholic statements and the 'anonymous Christianity' theory of Karl Rahner. And we shall face up to the question, 'Is there salvation (in a Christian sense) in other religions?'

Jesus Inclusively at the Centre

As with exclusivism, we need to start by thinking clearly about what inclusivism does not mean, when used in this particular debate. It is not, as it might sound, the complete opposite of exclusivism. In fact, it has, as we shall see, one very important belief in common. It is not saying that God's salvation will somehow eventually 'include' everybody, no matter what they have believed or how they have lived. That is *Not* universalism. Nor is it saying that our Christian *universalism* understanding of salvation can simply 'include', or *or syncretism* blend together with, all the other religions. That is *or pluralism* syncretism. Nor is this the view that we can 'include' all the great religions as equally valid in their own way as ways of salvation, with Christianity just one valid way among others. That is pluralism, which we shall come to in the next chapter. At this point, you might like to read again the definition of inclusivism given in the quotation at the start of Chapter 2.

The inclusive Christ

The one, central, and all-important point that exclusivism and inclusivism have in common is their commitment to the centrality of Jesus Christ. They are in agreement *The centrality* that Christ is the supreme and final revelation of God *of Christ* and that he is the one through whom ultimately people can and will be saved. However, whereas the exclusivist says that if Christ alone is the Truth and the Saviour, then that *excludes* all other faiths as vehicles of truth or salvation, the inclusivist argues that ultimately all truth is God's truth, wherever it is found. So Christ, who is *the* Truth, must therefore *include* all that is true in other faiths. All truth and goodness come from God, and therefore must also in some way be from and through Christ. So whatever truth and goodness we can discern in other faiths must be attributed to Christ who is in some way present and active within them, though in hidden ways. Christ is clearly and fully known within the Christian faith, but he also includes whatever is true in other faiths. Inclusivists tend to speak, therefore, in terms of *continuity* (rather than the exclusivist's discontinuity) between other faiths and Christianity. Or they see Christianity as the *fulfilment* of what is looked for, or hidden, or being prepared for, in other faiths. The exclusivist would draw a fairly sharp and unbroken line between the Christian faith and all other religions; the inclusivist would see a more soft, broken and porous line between them, with many points of common truth.[1]

Here is another definition of inclusivism, as given by the report of the Anglican Board of Mission and Unity (BMU), *Towards a Theology of Inter-Faith Dialogue:*

> As a result of the realisation that a great spiritual depth is found in many of the religious traditions of the world and that they show all the signs of persisting in the future, many theologians are turning to a more positive account of the place of other religions within a Christian understanding of the activity of God. While holding firmly to the belief that God was supremely manifest in Jesus, inclusivist theories also affirm the universal presence of God's Spirit through the whole of creation. God's saving power and presence is defined in the life and death and resurrection of Jesus, but is not confined to him. Through the Logos [i.e. the Word, of John 1], or his Spirit, God is operative beyond Christian culture, bringing salvation to other peoples and cultures who may not even know the name of Jesus. (Para. 18).[2]

As with exclusivism, there are different degrees of inclusivism among those who would identify with the term. We shall look at two major views.

i) *'Revelation – Yes; Salvation – No'.* First of all, there are those who are willing to agree that God has made his universal general revelation available to all human beings, and so other religions, simply because they reflect our humanity which is made in God's image, do include some truths of general revelation. That is not to say, of course, that everything they teach is true. And even where there is truth it may also be distorted and be understood differently from the biblical revelation. And in addition, many inclusivists would recognise that these elements of truth in other religions are mixed up also with degrees of demonic infiltration and human corruption which can be found in all religions – including Christianity as a religion. Nevertheless, the inclusivist wants to say that wherever people of other faiths believe something that is true, that can be affirmed and included within the work of Christ.

But this inclusivist viewpoint denies that there is any *saving* work of God in other religions as such. Other religions are not 'salvific'. That is, they would not accept that *Not salvific* God can be said to save people *through* those religions. So on this view, Christ still remains central and necessary for salvation, but other faiths may go a long way in preparing for Christ, through the truth they possess, or they may even be in some way provisional vehicles for the grace of God which is fully manifest only in Christ. As the BMU report expresses it, Jesus is 'the concrete historical manifestation of what is hidden in the depths of other religions'. That is, when people eventually are confronted with the gospel of Jesus, they recognise the full and saving truth which their previous religion contained or pointed to only in partial or hidden ways. They may say that Jesus fulfils what they were longing for. Or Jesus answers the questions the other religions raised but could not finally solve. So when they are saved by Christ, even though they experience conversion, there is some continuity with their religious past, not merely a total renunciation.

The difficulty here is in moving from what is undoubtedly true at the level of individual subjective religious experience to categorical 'blanket' statements about the objective relationship between the Christian faith with its biblical revelation claims, and other religious systems. Even at the level of personal testimony there is a very varied expression of how people view their present Christian identity and experience in comparison or contrast with their pre-Christian religious affiliation. I have spoken to Christians in India who describe their conversion from Hinduism

Personal testimony in the most disjunctive terms. That is, they felt (and continue to feel) it necessary totally to renounce what Hinduism stood for in their lives; they speak of being 'delivered' from it; often they have had to pay a very high social and familial cost for conversion; they are wary of all attempts to make Christian worship or theology more culturally Indian, since Indian culture is naturally so suffused with Hindu assumptions. But I have also spoken to Indian Christians who speak more positively of the way Christ has fulfilled all that Hinduism led them to search for but could not itself provide. They relish the discovery of points of continuity or similarity and they believe it to be missiologically and evangelistically important to stress such links. I understand that a very similar diversity of testimony is found among Christians who come from an Islamic background. The theological stance of inclusivism may be a way of giving formal expression to the second kind of personal experience. But it needs to recognise that actual experience of other faiths 'on the ground' is much more complex than a theologian's formula, and to allow room for those who view their pre-Christian world in a very different light.

ii) *'Anonymous Christians'*. Within the Roman Catholic church something of a revolution in attitude towards non-Christian religions took place in the Second Vatican Council (1962-1965). Previously, the dominant position throughout the centuries had been that salvation was exclusively available, not only through Christ alone, but also through the Roman Catholic church alone, as expressed in the saying of Origen (3rd century), *'extra ecclesiam, nulla salus'* ('outside the church, there is no salvation').[4] The Council, however, through a number of documents,[5] articulated a much more inclusivist view in which the grace of God was claimed to be operating in and through other religions because of God's desire to offer salvation to all human beings.[6] The following quotations illustrate this new attitude.

There are those who without any fault do not know anything about Christ or his church, yet who search for God with a sincere heart and, under the influence of grace, try to put into effect the will of God as known to them through the dictate of conscience: these too can obtain eternal salvation.[7]

The Catholic church rejects nothing which is true and holy in these religions. She has a sincere respect for those ways of acting and living, those moral and doctrinal teachings which may differ in many respects from what she holds and teaches, but which none the less often reflect the brightness of Truth which is the light of all men. But she proclaims, and is bound to proclaim unceasingly, Christ who is 'the way, the truth, and the life' (Jn 14:6). In him men find the fullness of their religious life and in him God has reconciled all things to himself (cf. 2 Cor 5:18-19).[8]

This official teaching coincided with the work of a major Roman Catholic theologian, Karl Rahner, who was an official adviser at the Second Vatican Council. He summarised his views in the form of four 'theses':[9]

i) *'Christianity understands itself as the absolute religion, intended for all men, which cannot recognise any other religion beside itself as of equal right.'* Thus, the centrality and finality of Christ is preserved. However, Christianity can only be this for people when it is actually encountered by them historically in a given context. Before that other religions have a legitimate place in God's saving purpose. Hence:
ii) *'Until the moment when the gospel really enters into the historical situation of an individual, a non-Christian religion... does not merely contain elements of a natural knowledge of God [i.e. general revelation]... It also contains supernatural elements arising out of the grace which is given to men as a gratuitous gift on account of Christ. For this reason a non-Christian religion can be recognised as a lawful religion... without thereby denying the error and depravity contained within it.'* It is important to see that such grace as Rahner sees in other religions is always grace won through Christ. Therefore,

those who respond to God's grace through their own religion are in fact responding, implicitly, to Christ. Hence:

iii) *'Christianity does not simply confront the member of an extra-Christian religion as a mere non-Christian but as someone who can and must be regarded... as an anonymous Christian.'* Thus, if there are 'anonymous Christians' (i.e. those who are related to Christ by implicit faith, but do not know or take that name for themselves) among other religions then:

iv) *'The church [is not] the exclusive community of those who have a claim to salvation but rather... the vanguard... and the explicit expression of what the Christian hopes is present as a hidden reality even outside the visible church.'*

Thus, to summarise Rahner's view, God's universal saving grace is so powerfully seeking people that those who have as yet had no contact with the Christian gospel are 'allowed' to find in their own religion 'a positive means of gaining a right relationship to God and thus for attaining salvation, a means which is therefore positively included in God's plan of salvation.'[10] He regards sincere non-Christians as 'anonymous Christians', in virtue of the grace of Christ which they have received and unwittingly responded to in their own faiths. Thus, people can be saved by God's grace and by Christ, without actually belonging to the visible Christian church. The sincere Hindu, for example, will be saved by Christ, but it is through the 'sacraments' of Hinduism that Christ saves him. He is in fact an 'anonymous Christian'.

Rahner's 'anonymous Christianity' has been the target of much debate and plenty of criticism. Many critics say that it is patronising towards people of other religions to think

Anonymous Muslims?

we are doing them a favour by regarding them as anonymous Christians. As Peter Cotterell puts it, 'The honorary granting of Christian citizenship to those who have not asked for it, and who have, in some cases, positively resisted it (as is true of both Muslims and Jews), savours of sheer imperialism.'[11] It is easy to imagine what Christian reaction would be if we were to be told by ardent representatives of Islam, that we are in fact 'anonymous Muslims'.

Furthermore, although Rahner does acknowledge that religions contain that which is distorted and in error, his approach seems on the whole much more positive towards religions than is deserved by their actual 'track record' in promoting human happiness and good relations on earth, let alone in providing eternal salvation. Again, Peter Cotterell makes the point well:

> The religions themselves are hopelessly idealised [sc. by inclusivism, and especially 'anonymous Christianity']. The world's religions are *not* kindly debating societies, but as those of us who have lived among them for any length of time will know, they are a morass of superstition, ignorance, exploitation, oppression, fear. And... this is as true of *Christianity* as a religion as it is true of any other religion. The horrors of Canaanite religion are still with us, the *shaman* still claims the power to manipulate his gods, witchcraft still flourishes, the credulous are exploited, human achievement is exalted, the rich are filled with yet more good things, and it is the poor who are sent empty away.
>
> The fact is that religions do not prepare their adherents for the revelation of Christ. Paradoxically, the closer any religion stands to Christianity, so higher is the barrier erected by it between its own adherents and the Christian revelation. If salvation is to be found by the adherents of these religions, it may well be found while they are still in them, but it will be found not because of them, but in spite of them.[12]

Is there salvation in other religions?

In the preceding discussion we have been talking about whether or not other religions can be means of salvation, even if ultimately salvation depends on the work of Christ. But actually, the very question itself, 'Is there salvation in other religions?' is very strange when considered from a biblical point of view. It seems to take for granted that salvation is something you get through a religion. It seems to have a built-in assumption that says, 'We've got salvation through our religion, but can people get salvation through other religions?'

But a major assertion of the whole Bible is that there is salvation in *no* religion. *Religion does not save anybody. God does.* And the Bible is fundamentally the story of what God has done in history to save his whole creation including humanity.

Salvation is a personal, costly, and historical achievement of God on our behalf, not the end result of religious activity on our part. Israelites in the Old Testament were not saved by their religion. *And neither are we Christians saved by ours!* Biblical religion is the response of worship and obedience to the God who has saved us. It is the way we express and live out our experience of salvation, not the means of achieving salvation. We are not saved because we are Christians; we are Christians because we are saved, and acknowledge Christ as our Saviour. Salvation, then, is what God has done, not what we have found or achieved by religion or any other means.

Salvation is what God has done

It is this fundamental fact about the Christian gospel – that it is good *news,* not a good idea; that it is the declaration of historical events by which God has intervened to save us from our sin – which exposes the inadequacy of all other religions. There is no salvation in them, not because they have nothing in common with Christianity in their *beliefs* (some do), but because they do not recount these *events* and therefore do not put people in touch with what God has already done to save them.

> However much theological and spiritual insight other religions may have, then, by definition they cannot encompass the gospel, because they do not tell the gospel story. So, while one may honour them as starting points for people, one cannot in love view them as finishing points. There is no salvation in them, not because they are somehow inferior as religions to the religion of Christianity, but because they are not witnesses to the deeds of the God who saves.[13]

How inclusive can you get?

Inclusivism, then, attempts to preserve the uniqueness and centrality of Christ, but shifts the focus away from an exclusive view of Christ or the church to a wider understanding of the action of God in and through other human faiths. It is attractive to many because it tries to preserve what most Christians still feel is the essence and heart of their faith (that the highest revelation and the true source of salvation is in Christ), and yet to be open-minded and open-armed to fellow human beings and their experiences and beliefs. Or, as the BMU report puts it, it means combining 'an inclusive approach to other faiths, with an exclusive loyalty to Christ'.

Often in arguments of this sort, the difficulty is knowing where you have to draw the line between what you can accept and what goes beyond what you think can be justified by the Bible. Personally, I can go a long way with those who, on the grounds of general revelation, affirm that all human religions embody some aspects of truth simply because we are humans and cannot escape from the God in whose image we are made. To that extent I can cautiously accept some of position (i) inclusivism, as explained above. On the other hand it seems to me that Paul's evaluation of such general knowledge of God in Romans 1 and 2 prohibits the idea that somehow humans can be saved by it. On the contrary, we have universally distorted the knowledge we have, and chosen to worship the created in the place of the Creator. All religions, therefore, share this duality that is inherent in the human condition: they include aspects of truth and they distort that truth, providing in a variety of ways mechanisms by which human beings can institutionalise their rebellion against God just as much as pursue their search for God.

Where to draw the line?

I reject, therefore, an inclusivism which wants to find salvation in other religions. That is where I draw a line because it seems to me that to go further than that is to start down a slippery slope that lands up in pluralism. In other words, an inclusivism which is too open-ended loses any logical or theological defence against those who are now pushing for complete relativism in religion. This is a charge against the inclusivists which is actually made from the other end of the spectrum by the out and out pluralists. They say that if the inclusivists follow the logic of their own argument they ought to arrive at a pluralist destination. Race, for example, who is a pluralist, highlights the tension between the two things that the inclusivists are trying to hold together:

A slippery slope

> Inclusivism proceeds on the basis of commitment to two equally
> binding convictions: the universal will of God to save, and the
> uniqueness of the revelation in Christ.[14]

Now both of these convictions can be supported as fully biblical affirmations, when you explain and understand them properly. Yet Race wonders if they can any longer be held together – at least in the way the inclusivist wants to. The one which Race chooses to throw out, of course, is the second (unique revelation in Christ), so that he can then feel free to affirm a pluralist universalism which becomes no longer biblical at all. But he argues that inclusivists will eventually have to acknowledge that they cannot hold the two beliefs together, and ought then to accept the inevitability of the pluralist stance. Inclusivists, naturally, refuse the invitation!

Inclusivism, then, is a difficult position to define precisely and defend adequately. Those who advocate it obviously want to steer between the rocks of narrowly dogmatic exclusivism (especially restrictivism), and the whirlpool of relativism and pluralism, *which they equally strongly reject*.[15] They want to hold on to the uniqueness of Christ, and yet to find legitimate theological space within an understanding of God's sovereignty for the existence of non-Christian religions. One inclusivist theologian, with whom I shared a public debate, put it like this: 'I want us to be able to sing our love-songs to Jesus without having to tell dirty stories about the faith of others.' I agreed, of course. We are not called upon to disparage other religions by highlighting their worst defects, unless we are willing to have the same treatment as regards the extremes and excesses of historical Christianity. However, I do not think it is possible to sing love-songs to Jesus in a way that is faithful to the New Testament without implicitly or explicitly excluding the truth-claims of other faiths that either have never had a place for him, or have quite consciously rejected the New Testament's claims regarding him. That is not to 'tell dirty stories'. It is simply to say that the biblical story, if true, is incompatible with other stories in relation to ultimate revelation and salvation.

I find myself, then, in some ways attracted to inclusivism because of the problem it is trying to avoid, and yet very uncomfortable with it because of the result it seems to lead to and the questionable theological bases on which it rests. And so, because of the range of ambiguity within the term, and especially its association with the 'anonymous Christianity' theory of Karl Rahner, I find myself still preferring the exclusivist account of the matter to the inclusivist,[16] and still wishing that better terminology could be found for the debate!

4

Jesus in Orbit: Pluralism

We now move in this chapter from those views of the relationship between Christianity and other faiths which maintain a fundamental affirmation of the uniqueness and centrality of Jesus Christ, to the pluralist viewpoint which regards Jesus as just one among many possible saving points of contact with God. As before, we shall try to think clearly about what pluralism does and does not mean, and then consider a number of objections to it. We shall look especially at what pluralism does to the Christian understanding of God, of Jesus, of the New Testament, and of worship.

Jesus in Orbit: Pluralism

In moving from the topics considered in the last two chapters to the theme of this one we are crossing a very large gap. The three positions, exclusivism, inclusivism and pluralism are not spaced out, as it were, at equal points along a grid. Rather, the major and most critical divide is between exclusivism-inclusivism on the one hand and pluralism on the other. *The great divide* Remember that the one thing exclusivism and inclusivism have in common is their affirmation of the centrality of Jesus Christ. Whether that is expressed in terms that primarily exclude the truth and salvation claims of other faiths, or in terms that seek to include the truth (and for some also the provisional saving potential) of other faiths, both positions claim to uphold the essential heart of Christianity, namely that Jesus Christ is ultimate Lord and Saviour and that all religious claims and beliefs must be judged in the light of Christ.

Though I have signalled my disagreement at various points in the last chapter, it still seems to me possible for fundamental loyalty to the uniqueness and finality of Christ to be held sincerely alongside views that could place one at different points between exclusivism and inclusivism. That is, people can adopt different theological positions (with varying degrees of biblical support) on the precise nature of God's action in and attitude to the religions of the world, while continuing to affirm that only in

71

Christ is God fully revealed and only by Christ are people saved.

A complete surrender

The shift to pluralism, on the other hand, requires either a complete surrender of the uniqueness of Christ, or such a radical redefinition of it that it loses all value. For the pluralist, Christ is quite definitely no longer central or ultimate in his or her understanding of religion. It is this critical and pivotal difference which means that, whereas I can regard inclusivism as a Christian option, even while regarding some aspects of it as theologically deficient or distorted, I cannot regard pluralism as a Christian option at all, inasmuch as it explicitly rejects that which is at the very heart of the Christian faith.

An important distinction

We need to remind ourselves of the point made in Chapter 1, that the word 'pluralism' is here being used in a strictly theological sense. It should not be confused with social plurality of religions. There is a vast difference between the simple *fact* of *social plurality*, within which we as Christians have to relate to other religions and cultures and to do so with love, tolerance and respect for fellow human beings, and the *ideology* of *religious pluralism*, with its relativist assumptions.

As we saw in Chapter 1, Christians in the West now find themselves living alongside communities of other faiths. They are thus experiencing the kind of plurality of religions that has been a fact of life, of course, for most non-Western Christian communities for centuries. It is perhaps typical of the 'blinkered' nature of western Christianity that western theologians tend to imagine that what is a new experience for them is a new phenomenon in the history of Christianity itself, when in fact it is as old as the New Testament. The first Christians lived in a world (the Greek and Roman civilisation) that was just as riddled with plurality of religions as our own, and yet they courageously bore witness to the uniqueness and universality of Jesus Christ in that context. It is certainly true to say that in the western world the 'sacred canopy' of Christian belief (to use Peter Berger's phrase) has been broken up by the awareness and presence of other cultures and religions. But neither changing social patterns, nor increasing and improved factual knowledge about other faiths, can change the objective truths of God's revelation. Such new circumstances may (indeed should) change the way we think and talk about how the gospel relates to those other faiths. *Historical* But the historical events upon which the Christian *events have* gospel is founded have not changed. And thus the truth *not changed* of the claim that Jesus of Nazareth was unique both as God incarnate and as the only Saviour is not something that has to be repeatedly modified because of changes in the social and religious contexts in which Christians happen to live in each generation. Either Jesus was God and still is, or he is not God and never has been. It is this theological issue we are concerned about here.

What pluralism means

As we have said, all the positions we have looked at up to now want to preserve the centrality of Christ himself – whether in exclusive or inclusive terms. Christ is the centre and the standard (norm) for all other faiths (the technical term for this position is *Christocentric* – i.e. placing Christ at the centre). Pluralists, however, argue that we should see only God at the centre of the religious universe, not Christ or Christianity (the technical term for this view is *theocentric,* from the Greek, *theos,* 'god'). So when you put the two terms together, you have *theocentric pluralism*, which means that all the religions, including Christianity, are related in some way to this 'God at the centre', but none of those religions and none of the 'gods' they name and claim, is actually in that central place. It is immediately clear that such a view does not accept that Jesus Christ can be identified in any way with this 'God at the centre' – a fundamental point which we shall come to below.

Now this is not merely 'religious syncretism'. Syncretism is the desire to blend and unite the best in all world religions into one future composite world faith. Syncretism is 'Pick 'n' Mix' religion. It assumes that some parts of some religions will have to be rejected, while keeping the best elements of all religions that are compatible with each other. Pluralism, on the other hand, is content to accept all the faiths, as wholes, as valid and complementary. They are said to be different responses to what is often called the one 'Ultimate Divine Reality' (another way of talking about 'God at the centre'). Even apparent contradictions between different religions can be seen as merely the result of our human limitations – we simply cannot grasp the whole truth. So you don't have to try to resolve those contradictions. Even if the beliefs of one religion are diametrically contradictory to those of another, you don't need to decide which is true and which is false, for according to pluralism they can all be 'true' at some more profound level of reality which we do not yet understand. Or they can be relatively and adequately true for their own adherents, but not absolutely true for all. It is a basic assumption of pluralism

No absolute truth that no single religious tradition can claim to have or to be 'the truth'. In fact, there is no absolute truth available to us through any religion. There are only partial understandings which are historically and culturally relative. So a theology of religious pluralism also goes along with a philosophy of relativism – i.e. the denial of any absolute truth.

Alan Race offers a definition of pluralism, or relativism, as follows:

> … the belief that there is not one, but a number of spheres of saving contact between God and man. God's revealing and redeeming activity has elicited response in a number of culturally conditioned ways throughout history. Each response is partial, incomplete, unique; but they are related to each other in that they represent different culturally focused perceptions of the one ultimate divine reality.[1]

Salvation can therefore be found in any or all faiths, including Christianity. But it is certainly not confined to Christianity. Christ and Christianity, instead of being the centre of the saving and revealing work of God, 'go into orbit' along with other faiths, as just one among many planetary responses to the gravitational pull of the sun of 'ultimate divine reality' at the centre of the religious universe. God as understood by Christians as revealed in Christ, is not to be identified as the 'sun at the centre'. As just one perception of deity, 'the Christian God' is to be regarded as simply one of a number of planets in orbit around it.

This astronomical way of describing this view comes from John Hick who is one of the leading exponents of this pluralist understanding of religions. Hick argues that Christians have to make such a radical shift in their whole religious understanding that it is like a 'Copernican Revolution' in theology. Copernicus was one of those early astronomers who proved that the earth was a planet of the sun, rather than *Planets in orbit* the sun going round the earth. People always used to believe that the earth stood still and everything revolved around it. That's what it looks like from here! It took an enormous adjustment for humanity (and especially the church) to be weaned from the apparently obvious 'fact' that the earth stands motionless at the centre of the universe, surrounded by other moving heavenly bodies, and to accept the actual truth that it is the sun which is the centre of our solar system and that the earth, along with other spinning planets, is revolving around it. It was no easy thing to accept our own relativity, i.e. to see that our earth which seems so central to ourselves is actually only one of several planets relative to a central sun.

Similarly, says Hick, it is not easy for Christians to see that while Jesus Christ may be central for their own faith and worship, he is not actually the centre of the whole religious universe. Only God is that. Christ is simply one among many who have borne valid witness to the divine reality and enabled people to come into some kind of saving contact with God.

> We have to realise that the universe of faiths centres upon *God* and not upon Christianity or any other religion. He is the sun, the originative source of light and life, whom all the religions reflect in their different ways.[2]

What's wrong with pluralism?

Superficially, pluralism can seem plausible and attractive. After all, it still talks about God and has Christ in the picture somewhere, so what more do you need? You are allowed to keep

Christ as the focus of your own religion, so long as you make room for the other 'planets' in the religious solar system. Isn't that fair enough? It also seems to relieve us of all that worry about what will happen to those who never hear the gospel of Christ. They have their own religion which puts them in touch with God, so that's all right then too. And most of all, it fits so perfectly with the 'supermarket mentality' that characterises the modern (and post-modern, but that's a different story) western mind, as we saw in the Introduction. However, underneath all these attractive features pluralism has some major implications that set it totally at odds with biblical Christianity and make it actually a particularly dangerous philosophy for Christians to toy with. My dominant criticisms are directed at what it does to our understanding of God, Jesus, the New Testament and the worship of Christians themselves.[3]

Pluralism reduces God to abstractions

Hick and his fellow pluralists, then, want us to adopt a form of 'pluralist theocentrism' – that is, we no longer put Christ or the church at the centre, but only God. However, one marked feature of this 'revolution' is that the *theos* ('god') who is finally left at the centre becomes utterly abstract. Clearly 'he' cannot be identified or named in terms of any particular deity known within the different world faiths, for they are all only partial responses to this mysterious being. In fact Hick is quite insistent on this. Names like Jahweh (Hick uses 'J'), Jesus, Vishnu, Allah, Brahman, etc., are simply human cultural constructs by means of which people within a particular religious community give expression to their experience of the divine. Whatever those believers may think or claim, the names of their gods are not to be identified with the actual divine reality. (It is important to realise that what pluralism does to Christianity it also does to *Humanly* all religions; none of them has access to the ultimate *constructed* truth about God as God really is.) Those names or *masks* concepts found in the various religions are like humanly constructed 'masks'[4] by which the divine is thought to be encountered by devotees of those religions. But none of them is ultimately true in the way their worshippers claim. Thus, for example, Hick says about the Jewish view of God: 'The concrete figure of Jahweh is thus not identical with the ultimate divine reality as it is in itself, but is an authentic face or mask or *persona* of the Transcendent in relation to one particular human community.' He then goes on to say that this is how he regards the ultimate names of deity in other religions, 'For precisely the same has to be said of the heavenly Father of Christianity, of the Allah of Islam, of Vishnu, of Shiva, and so on.'[8]

So one finds that the 'sun at the centre' is given other 'names' which are in fact not names at all but abstract 'undefinitions'. 'Ultimate Divine Reality' is Hick's favourite. Then you will often read of 'Transcendent Being', or even simply, 'The Real'. And if you ask what this 'Being' is like, you will be told that you cannot know. It is beyond description or knowing as it is in itself. But all the religions have some partial view of it through the 'lens' of their culturally particular religion.

By using this kind of language you can also avoid having to decide whether this divine being is personal or impersonal. This is very convenient, since that is precisely the point of conflict between, say, Hinduism and Christianity, and even within different schools of Hinduism. But the language of the pluralists certainly tends towards an *impersonal* view of deity. There is little of the living warmth of the biblical language of the personal characteristics of God. Most ordinary people find the abstract concepts of philosophers rather difficult to understand, and even more difficult to believe in for their salvation. As Newbigin has put it so strongly, why should we have to believe that an impersonal, undefinable abstraction has any better claim to be the centre of the religious universe than a known person who stands revealed in recorded history? Why should such an abstract philosophical concept be regarded as a more reliable starting point for discovering the truth and finding salvation than commitment to a personal God in Christ?[6]

Pluralism diminishes Jesus

The pluralists want us to be theocentric (God-centred) but to give up being Christocentric (no longer to have Christ at the centre). The trouble is that it seems impossible to do

God or Christ at the centre

that and stay within the framework of New Testament faith. There are some scholars, however, who try to drive a wedge between the fact that Jesus preached the kingdom of *God* (i.e. a theocentric proclamation), and the fact that the church preached *Jesus* (thus shifting the focus to a Christocentric proclamation which then became the church's dominant position). However this will not do. Certainly Jesus preached the kingdom of God – a very theocentric thing to do. But the kingdom of God, *as preached by Jesus*, centred on himself – who he was and what he had come to do. In fact it was precisely because he so persistently put himself at the centre of his teaching about God and about God's kingdom that Jesus aroused such hostility. There was nothing at all scandalous about simply being theocentric in Jewish society! God was at the centre of everybody's religious 'universe' in one way or another. But for a man to claim that Scriptures concerning the future work of God were fulfilled in himself, that he had power to forgive sins, that he was Lord over the Sabbath, that he was the Son of Man to whom eternal dominion would be given, and many other such claims (see next chapter), was simply blasphemy – and was indeed reckoned to be blasphemous by his contemporaries. That was why they crucified him – not for being theocentric, but for putting himself in that centre where they knew only God should be. Blasphemous it certainly was – unless of course it was true.

In the same way, the first Christians, who were Jews and therefore strict monotheists, already lived in a thoroughly theocentric universe. They were shaped to the core by the central affirmation of Jewish faith, 'Hear, O Israel: the LORD our God, the LORD is one: Love the LORD your God with all your heart and with all your soul and with all your strength' (Deut 6:4-5). But with considerable struggle and often at great personal cost, they deliberately put their contemporary, the man Jesus of Nazareth, right at the centre of that majestic Old Testament faith. They did so every time they made the crucial affirmation 'Jesus is Lord'. That did not mean they had given up or diluted their theocentrism. On the contrary, their faith in God at the centre of the religious universe was as strong as ever. But now it was filled out, redefined, and proclaimed in the light of their encounter with

God in the person and action of Jesus, the Christ. So Paul could write what is virtually an expansion of the great Jewish creed to include Jesus Christ alongside the Creator God.

> For us there is but one God, the Father, from whom all things came and for whom we live; and there is but one Lord, Jesus Christ, through whom all things came and through whom we live (1 Cor 8:6).

The New Testament writings are a constant reflection of the struggle by which the God-centred faith of the Old Testament was seen to be Christ-centred in reality. This was not a perversion, nor an exaggeration born out of human hero-worship. It was the calm conviction that Jesus of Nazareth, in the light of his life, death and resurrection, was indeed the centre and key to the whole redemptive work of God, past, present and future. He was at the centre of their theocentric religious universe because he was Immanuel, no less than *God with us*.

Jesus was the centre

It seems to me that the pluralist view cannot be reconciled with authentic Christianity, because to relativise Jesus Christ is to deny him. By 'relativising Jesus' I mean regarding him as only one among many great religious figures through whom we can know about God and find salvation. It means regarding him as one of the orbiting planets of world religions, not as the one and only absolute source of life and light as, for example, John 1 presents him.

A relativised Jesus?

If the New Testament is taken even as a reasonably reliable source, then it is unquestionable that Jesus made some astounding and absolute claims for himself. It is equally clear that his immediate followers in the early Christian church made similar claims concerning him, both explicitly in their preaching, and implicitly in their worship and prayer through his name.

So since biblical and historical Christianity makes such affirmations about Jesus, it follows that whatever kind of 'Christianity' is put into orbit around the 'sun of ultimate divine reality', it is not the 'Christianity' of Christ and his apostles.

Pluralists will reply that Jesus still remains central *for Christians* and that nothing need change that. As such, they say,

Jesus only for Christians? Jesus is the distinctive Christian gift to the inter-religious dialogue. But, we are told, we should only come to the dialogue table once we have renounced those absolute claims to the uniqueness or finality of Christ. For those claims are regarded by pluralists as arrogant and intolerant and therefore out of place in genuine dialogue. Jesus may be decisive and authoritative for those who have chosen to follow him (Christians), but he need not be imposed on others as unique or universal. Thus Race says: 'Jesus is "decisive", not because he is the focus of all the light everywhere revealed in the world, but for the vision he has brought in one cultural setting. ...Jesus would still remain central for the Christian faith.'[7] In other words, the great New Testament affirmation 'Jesus is Lord' is reduced to meaning, 'Jesus is Lord for us because we have chosen to regard him as such; his lordship is relative to our acceptance of him.' It no longer means, 'Jesus is objectively and absolutely the universal Lord to whom alone we submit and to whom ultimately all creatures in heaven and earth will bow.'

'Christ' is greater than Jesus Another way of making this point, a way which seems to combine a pluralist viewpoint with some aspects of inclusivism, is to say that while 'Jesus' is *the name* for Christians, 'Christ' may have other names in other faiths and cultures. This is the view of the Indian scholar Raimundo Panikkar.[8] He argues that Christ is not less than Jesus of Nazareth, but at the same time the Christian cannot say that Christ is only Jesus, for that reduces the Divine Mystery to being exhaustively present in Jesus of Nazareth. Each 'authentic name' enriches and qualifies that mystery. Others may call the mediator of the mystery Yahweh, Krishna, Allah or Buddha: for the Christian it can only be Christ, but this Christ must not be encapsulated in the historical Jesus of Nazareth. Jesus is Lord for Christians, but 'Christ is "the name above all names"'.[9] We thus end up with a kind of universalised Christ ('Christ' is somehow everywhere within all religions) but a relativised Jesus ('Jesus' was simply one among many manifestations of the 'Christ'). But this is in stark contrast to the actual affirmation of the New Testament in the text which is misused and misquoted above. For in Philippians 2 it is precisely the historical *Jesus,* in the full particularity of his incarnation, cross and resurrection, who is given 'the name that is above every name... that at the name of *Jesus* every knee should bow, in heaven and on earth and under the earth, and every tongue confess that *Jesus* Christ is Lord, to the glory of God the Father' (Phil 2:9-11). This allows no separation between the historical Jesus of Nazareth and the cosmic Lord Jesus Christ.

But even supposing we were to go along with the pluralist at this point and accept that Jesus is unique only in the sense that he is relatively special for Christians, but not the supreme Lord of all. We then have to ask what kind of 'gift to inter-faith dialogue' this relativised Jesus actually is. If Jesus Christ was not God incarnate, if he was not the final revelation of God and the completion of God's saving work for humanity, if he is not the risen and reigning Lord, then we are faced with two possibilities. Either, a) Jesus himself was mistaken in the claims he made concerning himself, in which case he was either sadly deluded or an arrogant boaster. Certainly, if his enormous claims were actually false, he would not be a worthy religious figure whom we could bring to the dialogue table with any confidence. We would need to apologise, not evangelise. Or, b) the church from its earliest period (including the generation of Jesus' own contemporaries who were the first witnesses to him) has grossly misunderstood him, inflated his claims, and exaggerated his importance. The pluralist requires us to accept that the church throughout its history (until its rescue by late twentieth century pluralist enlightenment) has propagated, lived by, and based all its hope upon, a massive self-deluded untruth. A deluded Jesus or a deluded church, or both. This seems to be the unavoidable implication of the pluralists' insistence on relativising Jesus.

A deluded Jesus? Or a deluded church?

The dismal results of this view are quickly clear. A.G. Hunter, for example, argues that Jesus was in fact not more than human, but was elevated to divine status only by the church and installed in the Trinity only at the Council of Chalcedon. Somehow Hunter simply *knows* that it was 'psychologically and religiously impossible for Jesus [to have claimed divinity] and it is historically false to say that he did.'[10] When you can be so confidently and dogmatically negative about the 'historical' Jesus, you have to be equally negative and uncertain about what value he has for faith: 'What emerges,' Hunter concludes, 'is that though we are agreed that Jesus is at the heart of our faith as Christians, it is hard to find any clear consensus as to the precise delineation of his importance.'[11] If such paralysed agnosticism is all we are left with, is it worth contributing to religious dialogue at all? Is that what representatives of other world faiths want to hear from us? If, as pluralists say, we have to relativise Jesus before we can come to the dialogue, then we had better not come at all. All we have to bring with any integrity would be a repentant confession that we belong to a worldwide faith which throughout the whole of its history has had an illusion and a falsehood at its fundamental heart and core.

Pluralism treats the New Testament as 'myth'

It seems, then, that the pluralist position regarding Jesus cannot be reconciled with the New Testament on any face-value reading of it. So, it can only be offered as a 'Christian' option by means of a radical re-interpretation of central New Testament teaching in terms of *myth*. In Chapter 1, when we were considering the theological aspect of the debate, I pointed out that treating the New Testament as myth and advocating religious relativism or pluralism tend to go together. I tried to explain some of the technical terms involved in this argument. You might want to check those points out again on pp 24-31. At this point I want only to add three more comments on the matter.

First, if you decide to interpret the New Testament as myth you *Gagging the* have already ruled out from the start even the *witnesses* possibility of the New Testament writers ever asserting anything ontological about Jesus. 'Ontological', remember, means statements that claim to describe who and what he actually *is* in his own being. The mythic view simply assumes that whatever these people who actually knew Jesus asserted about his person or nature is to be taken as myth, that is, as 'story language' relating only to his function and his relationship to them (the New Testament authors) or to us. But just suppose that those early witnesses to Jesus actually did wish, consciously

and deliberately, to make ontological statements about Jesus.
Suppose they believed such affirmations to be objectively true,
(even when all allowance has been made for figures of speech and
the inadequacy of all human language). The mythic interpreter
will simply not be listening, for he has already decided in advance
on the basis of his modern world-view that all such statements
cannot be taken as descriptions of any objective reality (what
Jesus truly is), but only as subjective, confessional, 'love-
language' (what Jesus means to me).

Second, treating the New Testament as myth overlooks
the importance of its emphasis on history. It ignores the *Ignoring*
contrast between the world of known first-century *history*
mythical religions and the strongly historical affirmations of the
early Christians about Jesus of Nazareth. It is sometimes asserted
that the first Christian witnesses had no other way of expressing
what Jesus had meant for them or what they believed he had done
for them, except through the medium of the mythical world-view
of their day. I find this totally unconvincing. The first-century
world was awash with mythical and mystical religions, but the
New Testament preachers and writers made their assertions about
Jesus and his significance on the solid basis of historical events
which had been witnessed and attested by contemporaries who
knew him. Sometimes, indeed, it is clear that they were making
these historical statements and claims about Christ in deliberate
opposition to mythical ideologies, as in Colossians and 1 John.
The point is succinctly put in 2 Peter 1:16. 'We did not follow
cleverly invented stories when we told you about the power and
coming of our Lord Jesus Christ, but we were eye-witnesses of
his majesty.'

Third, this mythic re-interpretation ends up
allowing its adherents to assert the opposite of what   *Turning the*
the New Testament actually says, while still claiming   *text upside*
to be interpreting the New Testament itself. A fairly   *down*
typical piece of John Hick's writing should illustrate this. After
arguing that the incarnation is 'a mythological idea, a figure of
speech, a piece of poetic imagery', he goes on from that 'insight'
to draw the following conclusions:

When we see the Incarnation as a mythological idea applied to Jesus to express the experienced fact that he is our sufficient, effective and saving point of contact with God, we no longer have to draw the negative conclusion that he is man's one and only effective point of contact with God. We can revere Christ as the one through whom we have found salvation, without having to deny other points of reported saving contact between God and man. We can commend the way of Christian faith without having to discommend other ways of faith. We can say that there is salvation in Christ without having to say that there is no salvation other than in Christ.[12]

But that last point, of course, is precisely what the New Testament *does* say!

Pluralism renders Christian worship idolatrous

Religious pluralists say that Jesus cannot stand at the centre of the religious universe. He cannot be equated or identified with the God (however described) at the centre. We must not look at Jesus 'from above', so to speak, as God incarnate, but rather see him as essentially one of us (which he was of course) and do our 'Christology from below'. There are many shades of opinion among scholars who prefer this approach, but in the end what it means is that, whatever else Jesus may have been, he was ultimately not more than human. Certainly he was not God incarnate in any ontological sense. He may have been a vehicle or agent of God's activity for revelation and salvation, but only as a man. That is, he may have been one of those exceptionally special human beings through whom the rest of us can come to a deeper and clearer understanding of God, but the language about him being 'of God, with God or from God' is simply the understandable exaggeration that gives voice to faith and adoration and gratitude.

Many who take this view would agree that Jesus was unique in some sense: for example, in the depth of his own relationship with God and the extent to which he mediated God to others including ourselves. But they would see this as a uniqueness of degree, not of essence. God may have been very specially present and active through Jesus of Nazareth, but Jesus was not (and therefore is not) God. He cannot stand at the centre of the religious universe but, even in his

A uniqueness of degree

uniqueness as defined, he must go into orbit around the centre along with other great religious figures who all have their own unique features also.

The more I reflect on this view, the more surprised I am at how reluctant its advocates seem to be to draw the ultimate conclusion from it, which seems quite inescapable. And that is, that Christianity is, and always has been, the worst form of idolatry ever practised on earth.[13] The most serious charge which Jews and Muslims[14] have levelled against Christians all through the centuries would actually be true: we have elevated a human being to the place of God and have worshipped him there. For that is what we do, and have been doing ever since the book of Acts. We ascribe to Jesus honour and glory that belongs only to God; we call on his name in prayer as God; we call him Lord and refuse to acknowledge any other; we apply to him the most solemn Scriptures that Israel used concerning Yahweh; we sing to him songs of worship and praise that were originally sung to Yahweh, and have made up bookfuls of our own. All this we have done for two thousand years but with no justification at all, if the pluralists are right. For, no matter how remarkable he was, no matter what God did in and through him, if Jesus was not more than a man, then the whole Christian faith and all the generations of Christian worship have been a monstrous idolatry.

Conclusion

So we arrive at the end of the pluralists' road. At best, 'Christ' becomes so universal as to be of no real value except as a symbol. At worst, he is exposed as an idol for those who worship him, and as dispensable by those who don't.

5

Jesus and the Bible

It is time to turn from our survey of the different viewpoints on religions to see how a closer look at the Bible can help us to think more clearly about the question of the uniqueness of Jesus. We shall spend more time in the Old Testament than in the New, which may seem strange. But the reason is that we have to understand the uniqueness of Jesus by seeing him in the way that he saw himself. Only when we make an effort to do that, and then to see him in the way his first followers saw him, again in the light of their Old Testament Scriptures, will we be thinking clearly about the uniqueness of Jesus. In this chapter, then, we shall look at how the Old Testament prepares us for Jesus, by helping us grasp the seriousness of sin and the need for a 'big' salvation, by showing us the unique way God worked through Israel, and by showing us the uniqueness of God himself, as Yahweh.

Jesus and the Bible

Who did Jesus think he was and what did he think he had come to do? We look to the New Testament, of course, to find an answer to these questions. However, the New Testament immediately directs our attention to the Hebrew Scriptures that Jesus himself knew and loved, which we now call the Old Testament in the light of him. Indeed the opening verses of the canonical New Testament, in Matthew 1, call Jesus the son of David and the son of Abraham, and take the reader through a quick action replay of the whole Old Testament in the form of Jesus' genealogical ancestry. It is as if Matthew were saying to us, 'If you want to know who Jesus was and is, you must see him in the light of *this* story, as the fulfilment of the promises made to *this* people, as the arrival of *this* God among us to save us from our sins.'

So without the Old Testament you cannot understand Jesus. It is from the Hebrew Scriptures that we will gain insight into Jesus' own self-understanding, sense of unique identity and mission, because that is where he himself drew these things from.[1]

Unfortunately, many discussions about the significance of Jesus Christ within the context of world religions virtually cut him off from these historical and scriptural roots and speak of him as 'the founder of a new religion'. Now, of course, if by that is meant merely that Christianity as a worldwide religion historically goes

The founder of a new religion?

back to Jesus and then became a separate religion from Judaism within which it was born, then that may be superficially true. But certainly Jesus had no intention of launching another 'religion' as such. Who Jesus was and what he had come to do were both already long prepared for through God's dealings with the people he belonged to and through their Scriptures. That is where we must begin if we are to get our own view of his uniqueness straight also. What then does the Old Testament have to tell us that is significant for thinking clearly about the uniqueness of Jesus Christ?

Creation, sin and salvation[2]

Some of the most fundamental parts of the biblical world-view are laid down in its first few chapters – Genesis 1-11. It has been said that any human world-view consciously or unconsciously operates to answer four fundamental questions that are found in all cultures:

1   *Who are we?* (i.e. what does it mean to be human beings?)
2   *Where are we?* (i.e. what is the universe and why does it exist?)
3   *What has gone wrong?* (i.e. what is the real reason for all the evil and suffering in the world?)
4   *What is the solution?* (i.e. how can things be put right again?)[3]

The first three questions are answered in Genesis 1-11 (and further refined in the rest of the Bible as well, of course), while the answer to the fourth comprises the rest of the Bible's whole story of salvation, from Abraham (Genesis 12), through the cross and resurrection of Jesus, to the new creation at his second coming (Revelation 21-22).

The Bible begins, (in Genesis 1-2), by setting out the basic stage upon which the whole drama of earthly history is played – namely the creation framework. This has *Who and where are we?* a kind of triangular structure comprising the creator God, the earth, and the human race, each dynamically related to the other two. Thus questions 1 and 2 are answered: *Who are we?* We are creatures of the living personal God, made in that God's own image and therefore unique among the animals in our relationship to him. *Where are we?* We inhabit a world created by the same God and declared by God to be 'good', and we have been given delegated authority to manage the earth and all it contains.

The Bible then goes on (in Genesis 3-11), in answering question 3, to show how all three relationships within this framework – between God and humanity, between God and the earth and between humanity and the earth – have been fractured and distorted by evil. The account of **What has** the human rebellion, in its profound simplicity in **gone wrong?** Genesis 3 and the following narratives up to the Tower of Babel in Genesis 11, portray a world in which everything has gone wrong. Human beings are estranged from God and driven from his presence. The earth is subjected to God's curse and resists the dominion and stewardship of humanity. Human beings are in conflict with each other, at every level, from the corruption and inequality of sexual relations since the fall, through family friction, to social arrogance, violence and corruption. Sin entered into and affects every dimension of human life, spiritual, intellectual, physical and social. Worse still, sin accumulates and seems to intensify as the generations follow one another, so that sin and evil are woven into the historical and cultural structures of the world we are born into. The result is a world of individuals and nations scattered under God's curse and divided among themselves.

The Bible then gives us an assessment of the human predicament which is radical and comprehensive in its scope. This means that if God has got any answer **The solution** to question 4, it has to be as big as the problem set by question 3. In other words, it is the Old Testament's realism and honesty about the nature of sin which shows us what salvation has to be and that only God can achieve it. If we had space to embark on a full account of the Old Testament concept of salvation, we would indeed find that it too is exceedingly broad and deep – sufficient to cope with all the effects of sin in creation. It is personal and social, spiritual and physical, political and economic, human and ecological, local and cosmic, present and future. God as

Saviour meets every dimension of human need, and indeed intends to mend his whole creation. Thus, when we bring the Old Testament to bear on the issue of different religious claims, the first thing that happens is that we are prevented from getting away with facile and superficial concepts of salvation, because it shows up the depth and scale of human need and guilt. We need a saving solution that goes to the depths of our real problem as sinners.

Pluralist vagueness

I find it a frustrating exercise reading the work of religious pluralists because they tend to be so vague and inadequate on what salvation actually *is*. That is, there is no clarity as to what we need to be saved from, or what being saved may actually mean for us. And that in turn seems to me largely because they ignore the Old Testament's insight on the nature and seriousness of sin. Wilfred Cantwell Smith, for example, can speak of God 'saving' through all religions by using phrases like 'enabling a truly moral life', 'living with a more than mundane reference colouring one's goals', 'keeping the forces of despair and meaninglessness at bay'. It is true that salvation in its biblical sense will do all of these, but more as by-products, not as the essence of salvation in itself. John Hick talks about 'salvific transformation', which is achieved within all the major religious traditions, at least by their 'saints' – a saint being 'one in whom the transformation of human existence from self-centredness to Reality-centredness [?] is so much more advanced than in the generality of us'.[4] The criteria he suggests for assessing whether this has taken place, however, are entirely related to life in this world (which is, of course, also a concern of biblical salvation), but have little if anything to say about what may or may not lie beyond death. This is hardly surprising since the religions differ most markedly in what they envisage for human beings in the face of death.[5]

Other pluralists reject the idea of any radical fracture in the relationship between God and humanity such as the story of the Fall portrays. Once that basic problem – the broken relationship between personal human beings and the personal Creator God –

is overlooked, minimised or denied altogether, then salvation can be whatever you like, depending on your personal or cultural preference as to the solutions to the wide range of other human needs. *Salvation is whatever you like* The supermarket is back: you get whatever salvation your religion is able to pay for.

One of the best critiques of this vagueness over what salvation is comes from the pen of Carl Braaten, and is worth quoting at length:

> Christian theologians are debating the question whether or not there is salvation in other religions, and taking sides on the issue, without first making clear the model of salvation they have in mind. ...What is the salvation that theologians expect to find or not to find in other religions? Most of the debate so far has taken us nowhere, because vastly different things are meant by salvation. If salvation is whatever you call it, there is no reason for a Christian to deny that there is salvation in other religions...

Braaten then goes on to list a whole range of candidates for the label 'salvation', including illumination, union with the divine, equality, physical health, peace, justice, etc. He shows how all the religions and even the non-religious philosophies of the world have something to offer on these hopes and desires. But while the full-orbed biblical teaching on God's saving work for humanity does include such wide dimensions, they are not the heart of the matter. For the basic problem is human alienation from the living and life-giving God resulting in death.

Braaten continues:

> On a theological level salvation is not whatever you want to call it, the fulfilment of every need or the compensation for every lack... Salvation in the Bible is *The defeat of death* a promise that God offers the world on the horizon of our expectation of personal and universal death. The gospel is the power of God unto salvation because it promises to break open the vicious cycle of death... We cannot derive a final meaning for life on this side of death. We can gain the partial salvation we are willing to pay for, but none of these techniques of salvation can succeed in buying off death.

Salvation in the New Testament is what God has done to death in the resurrection of Jesus. Salvation is what happens to you and me and the whole world in spite of death... The story of salvation is a drama of death and resurrection, whatever other human, personal and social problems the word might take on. ...Since death is what separates the person from God in the end, only that power which transcends death can liberate the person for eternal life with God. This is the meaning of salvation in the biblical Christian sense.

Theologians who speak of salvation in the non-Christian religions should tell us if it is the same salvation that God has promised the world by raising Jesus from the dead. The resurrection gospel is the criterion of the meaning of salvation in the New Testament sense. When Christians enter into dialogue with persons of other religions, they must do their utmost to communicate what they mean by the assertion that Jesus lives and explain how this gospel intersects the hopes and fears of every person whose fate is to anticipate death... A Christology that is silent about the resurrection of Jesus from the dead is not worthy of the Christian name and should not be called Christology at all.[6]

It needs to be pointed out, in case these extracts give a wrong impression, that it is clear from the rest of the context of what Braaten says that he is not peddling a 'pie in the sky when you die' caricature of salvation, i.e. something which only counts after death. He quite agrees that the Bible has plenty to say about the present experience and reality of salvation in this life. Nor does he exclude the physical, social and environmental dimensions of salvation, which are certainly part of the Old Testament's vision of full salvation. But he rightly insists that unless the fundamental alienation of humanity from God, which the Bible calls death and attributes to sin, is dealt with, all other aspects of salvation remain ultimately cosmetic. And he rightly emphasises that the heart of the matter is resurrection – the historical resurrection of Jesus and the promised resurrection to eternal life of those who believe in him. Resurrection is the crowning New Testament answer. But it is the Old Testament which shows us the seriousness and complexity of the question.

The uniquess of Israel

Having 'set the question' by its description of the human predicament in Genesis 1-11, the Bible goes on to show how God began providing a solution, first through the call of Abraham and the creation of Israel as his people, beginning at Genesis 12. God's covenant with Abraham makes it very clear that what God has in mind is blessing for all nations (Gen 12:3; 18:18, etc.). Having shown that the effects of sin are universal (all nations are implicated in the story of human rebellion illustrated by the Tower of Babel in Genesis 11), the narrative now shows us that God's redemptive intention is equally universal (all nations will be blessed through Abraham). But at the same time, it shows us that the way God chose to achieve that goal was through a very particular historical means – the nation of Israel.

The Bible is quite clear that God's action in and through Israel was unique. Now this does not mean that God was not involved and active in the histories of other nations. The Old Testament explicitly asserts that he was.[7] It does mean that only in Israel did God work within the terms of a covenant of redemption, initiated and sustained by his grace. Amos was very well aware of God's moral and historical sovereignty over the other nations (see Amos 1-2; 9:7). But about Israel he asserts in God's name, 'You only have I chosen, of all the families of the earth' (Amos 3:2 – a fact, incidentally, which spelt no privileged immunity for Israel, but rather, says Amos, exposed them all the more to God's punishment). Deuteronomy says that Israel had experienced God's redemption (the Exodus) and God's revelation (at Mt Sinai) in a way that was unparalleled among any other nation in the whole span of time and space (Deut 4:32-34). Isaiah went on to tell Israel that it was because of their unique historical experience of Yahweh that they were qualified to bear witness to *Yahweh's* uniqueness as the only living God (Is 43:8-13). Even the 'holiness' of Israel was a means of expressing their uniqueness. It meant being set apart by God for his special purpose through them in the midst of the nations (Ex 19:5-6; Lev 20:26; Num 23:9; Deut 7:6).

To emphasise this truth about Israel does not take away from the other truth, namely that God's purpose through them was ultimately universal in scope. Israel only existed at all because of God's desire to redeem people from every nation. But in his sovereign freedom he chose to do so by this particular and historical means. The tension between the universal goal and the particular means is found throughout the Bible and cannot be reduced to either pole alone. What it comes down to is that while God has every nation in view in his redemptive purpose, in no other nation did he act as he did in Israel, for the sake of the nations. That was their uniqueness, which can be seen to be both exclusive (no other nation experienced what they did of God's revelation and redemption), and inclusive (they were created, called and set in the midst of the nations for the sake of the nations).

Now when we look at Jesus and ask what he achieved, we have to remember that he completed what God had already begun to work out through Israel. As we noted briefly above, this is precisely what the New Testament does in its opening chapter. Matthew begins his Gospel with his list of the ancestors (genealogy) of Jesus, which may seem to us an obscure and not very attention-grabbing way to begin the greatest story ever told. What the genealogy meant for the Jewish readers Matthew had in mind, however, was to remind them of their own story. It is a schematic genealogy reflecting each major period of Israel's history in the Old Testament. And what Matthew is saying to the reader is, 'If you really want to know who this Jesus is, you have to see him as the completion of *this* story.' Jesus as a historical, particular man has to be understood against the background of a historical, particular people. His uniqueness is linked to theirs.

Jesus completes the story

But we can go further than simply noting how Jesus brings the unique story of Old Testament Israel to its climax and completion. We have to reckon with the vitally important fact that the New Testament presents him to us as *the Messiah*: Jesus, the Christ. And the Messiah *was* Israel. That is, he represented and personified Israel. The Messiah was the completion of all that Israel had been put in the world for – i.e. God's self-revelation

Jesus embodied the mission

and his work of human redemption. The Messiah fulfilled the mission of Israel, which was to bring blessing to the nations. For this reason too, Jesus shares in the uniqueness of Israel. In fact, he was the whole point and goal of it. What God had been doing through no other nation, God now completed through no other person than the Messiah, Jesus of Nazareth. The paradox is that precisely through the narrowing down of his saving action to this unique, singular man, Jesus, God opened the way to making his saving grace available universally to all nations, which was his purpose from the beginning when he made that promise to Abraham.

It had been a mystery all through the Old Testament ages *how* God could bring about for Abraham what he had promised him – namely blessing to all nations. Paul saw this clearly and expounds it in Ephesians 2-3 and Galatians 3 especially. *A mystery* What the Gentile nations did not have before, because it *solved* was at that time limited to Israel, is now available to them in the Messiah Jesus. It is significant how regularly Paul inverts the normal order and puts Christ before Jesus in these passages. It is not accidental; Paul is making a point. It is precisely because the Messiah has come in the person of Jesus of Nazareth that the Old Testament hope of redemption is fulfilled in him (cf. Luke 1:33, 54f,68-79; 2:25-32, 38; 24:21ff), and also that redemption can now be extended to include people from all nations who are 'in the Messiah' through faith. It is worth quoting some of his key texts in full:

> He redeemed us in order that the blessing given to Abraham might come to the Gentiles through Christ Jesus, so that by faith we might receive the promise of the Spirit (Gal 3:14).

> You [Gentiles] are all sons of God through faith in Christ Jesus, for all of you who were baptised into Christ have clothed yourselves with Christ. There is neither Jew nor Greek, slave nor free, male nor female, for you are all one in Christ Jesus. If you belong to Christ, then you are Abraham's seed and heirs according to the promise (Gal 3:26-29).

> Remember that formerly you who are Gentiles ... at that time you

were separate from Christ, excluded from citizenship in Israel, and foreigners to the covenants of the promise, without hope and without God in the world. But now in Christ Jesus you who were once far away have been brought near through the blood of Christ (Eph 2:11-13).

... the mystery of Christ, which was not made known to men in other generations as it has now been revealed by the Spirit to God's holy apostles and prophets. This mystery is that through the gospel the Gentiles are heirs together with Israel, members together of one body, and sharers together in the promise in Christ Jesus (Eph. 3:4-6).

Unquestionably, then, there is a universal dimension to Paul's gospel, because of its roots in the Abraham covenant and its promise to 'all nations'. But it is firmly based on an exclusive foundation – only through the Messiah Jesus, just as it had previously been only through Israel. The uniqueness of Jesus is thus bound to the uniqueness of Old Testament Israel because both are the expressions of the unique saving work of God in history.

The uniqueness of Yahweh

There can be no more powerful affirmation in the Old Testament than the claim that Yahweh alone is truly God. This *Yahweh, the only God* indeed was the lesson that Israel were to expected to learn from their unique experience of his revelation and redemption. Thus after Deuteronomy 4:32-34 has affirmed the unparalleled experience of Israel, verses 35 and 39 go on to draw the consequences:

You were shown these things so that you might know that the LORD [i.e. Yahweh] is God; beside him there is no other ... Acknowledge and take to heart this day that the LORD is God in heaven above and on the earth below. There is no other.

It is important to realise that in the Old Testament this monotheistic faith is not merely a matter of arithmetic. That is, what Israel were to learn from their encounter with God in history was not merely that there was only one deity, not many. The point rather was *who* that God was. *Yahweh is God*. Therefore God is being defined in terms of the nature, character and actions of Yahweh, and especially in terms of his faithfulness to his promises and his great power to save and deliver his people. This too is the ringing declaration of the great prophecies in Isaiah 40-55. Read especially Isaiah 40:12-31; 43:10-12; 45:5, 22-24, and hear the strength of the claim that Yahweh is utterly beyond comparison. He is unique as God because he is in reality the only God, and therefore he is in sovereign control of history from beginning to end. The future belongs to Yahweh as much as the past.

Yahweh, the expected God

A very important ingredient in Old Testament Israel's hopes for the future was the conviction that at some point in their future (often phrased in the prophets as 'in that day', or 'in those days') Yahweh God himself would come and take action in the world, bringing both redemption and judgement. Isaiah 35, for example, announces 'Your God will come' (v4), and then goes on to list the signs and blessing that will be proof of his coming: the blind would see, the deaf hear, the lame walk and the dumb speak (v5f). Jesus himself pointed to these signs in his reply to the questioning disciples of John the Baptist. But if these things were now taking place, what did that mean about the identity of Jesus? (Mt 11:4-6).

In other places in the Old Testament, the promise that God himself would 'take over' is linked without explanation to the expected coming and rule of a messianic figure. This is clearest in Ezekiel 34. There God, in response to the failure of Israel's historical kings ('shepherds'), promises a restoration of full divine government ('I will shepherd the flock with justice', v16), but at the same time promises the rule of a future 'David' (v23f). When Jesus claimed to be the 'good shepherd' (Jn 10:11, 14), or to be the one whom even David called Lord (Mt 22:41-46), again the question arises: who had really come?

The Old Testament closes with the warning that Yahweh himself would come, but that he would be preceded by 'Elijah'

(Mal 4:5). In the light of this text, Jesus could declare that this prophecy about 'Elijah' was fulfilled in John the Baptist. But then, if 'Elijah' was to precede the coming of God himself, and John the Baptist was 'Elijah', who must Jesus be? The expected sequence was: 'Elijah, then Yahweh'. Everybody knew that they had heard John first, and then Jesus had come. So Jesus *who*? 'If you are willing to accept it,' said Jesus, when he made the statement about John (Mt 11:14). The difficulty of accepting what he was saying was probably not so much the fact that he identified John with 'Elijah', as to what that would then mean for the identity of Jesus himself. For those who *were* willing to accept it, it meant beyond doubt that God himself had indeed come in the person of Jesus of Nazareth, to bring in the new age of his kingdom and salvation.

Who must Jesus be?

Yahweh and Jesus

Very soon after the death and resurrection of Jesus we find the early church referring to him and addressing him in terms which had previously applied only to Yahweh in their Scriptures. They called him Lord, the Greek word *Kyrios* being the one regularly used in the Greek version of the Old Testament for the divine name Yahweh. They 'called on his name' in worship and prayer. That was a phrase used in the Old Testament for invoking the presence and power of God in worship (e.g. Ps 116:12f, 17). Stephen at the point of death declared that he saw Jesus standing at the right hand of God sharing in his divine glory (Acts 7:55). Paul, in an act of instinctive evangelism, called on the Philippian jailer to 'believe in the Lord Jesus', if he wanted to be saved (Acts 16:31). Elsewhere he could theologically justify such confidence by quoting Joel 2:32, 'Everyone who calls on the name of the LORD will be saved.' Joel was unquestionably referring to Yahweh. Paul, just as unquestionably, was referring to Jesus Christ as the agent of God's salvation for Jew and Gentile alike (Rom 10:13). In John's Gospel, Jesus repeatedly uses 'I am' statements, climaxing in the claim in John 8:58 that 'before Abraham was born, I am'. There is no doubt that this intentionally echoes the similar 'I am' statements of Yahweh in the book of Isaiah[8] and the

Jesus at the right hand of God

implication was not lost on Jesus' Jewish hearers – they set out to stone him for blasphemy.

Possibly the most remarkable identification of Jesus with Yahweh comes in Philippians 2:5-11, the hymn of Christ's humility and exaltation. It is widely agreed that these verses were probably not originally composed by Paul, but were part of a Christian hymn which he incorporates here to make his point. They are thus very early evidence of Christian convictions about Jesus. The hymn finishes by saying that God has given to Jesus 'the name that is above every name' (v 9). In biblical terms, that could only mean the name that belonged to God – Yahweh himself, the name so often simply rendered 'LORD' in the Old Testament. So the next verse probably means to combine that implied name with the name Jesus itself. 'At the name belonging to Jesus'... there will be universal acknowledgement of his Lordship.

> ...that at the name of Jesus every knee should bow,
>> in heaven and on earth and under the earth,
> and every tongue confess that Jesus Christ is Lord,
>> to the glory of God the Father.

We are so familiar with this (from a well-known hymn!) that we perhaps are not aware that in fact this is a partial quotation of words which were originally spoken *by Yahweh* about himself, from Isaiah 45:21-24. And in that context the point of the words was to underline Yahweh's uniqueness as God and his unique ability to save.

> There is no God apart from me,
>> a righteous God and a Saviour;
> there is none but me.

> Turn to me and be saved, all you ends of the earth;
>> for I am God, and there is no other.

> By myself I have sworn,
>> my mouth has uttered in all integrity
>> a word that will not be revoked:

Before me every knee will bow;
by me every tongue will swear.

They will say of me, 'In the LORD alone are
rightousness and strength.'

This declaration by God comes in the most unambiguously monotheistic section of the whole Old Testament. The magnificent prophecies of Isaiah 40-55 assert again and again that

Jesus is as unique as Yahweh

Yahweh is utterly unique as the only living God in his sovereign power over all nations and all history, and in his ability to save. This early Christian hymn in Philippians 2, therefore, by deliberately selecting a Scripture from such a context and applying it to Jesus, is affirming that Jesus is as unique as Yahweh in those same respects. This is clear from the way the 'name' of Jesus is inserted at the crucial point where Yahweh would otherwise have been understood. Jesus *is* Lord, and will ultimately be recognised and acknowledged as such by all.

Another interesting factor here is the surrounding religious contexts of both texts. In both cases, Isaiah 45 and Philippians 2, it is actually religious plurality. In Philippians, the uniqueness of Jesus is asserted in the midst of the religious plurality of the Greek and Roman world of the 1st century AD. But it uses the same language and terms as the uniqueness of Yahweh himself had been asserted in the midst of the pluralistic, polytheistic environment of Babylon in the 6th century BC. I question, therefore, whether the rediscovered (but not new) religious plurality of the 20th century AD gives us any adequate reason for departing from affirmations made in both Testaments in similar contexts. At least we should be aware that if we insist on relativising Jesus out of deference to surrounding religious plurality, we take leave not only of the New Testament witness to him, but also jettison the Old Testament foundations on which it was built.

Jesus and the earliest witnesses

Paul's letter to the Philippians was probably written during his first imprisonment in Rome, somewhere around AD 60. If the text we have just considered (Phil 2:5-11) was indeed a Christian hymn that Paul quotes and incorporates in his letter, then it was obviously composed and circulating even before that. In other words, the incredibly exalted language used about Jesus, applying to him Old Testament texts used about (and even by) Yahweh himself, had become part of the worshipping life of the earliest Christian communities within a few decades of the death of Jesus. In fact it was happening within what would have been his own lifespan, since he died relatively young. Those who wrote and sang such words were the contemporaries of Jesus, people of his own generation.

And we can go back further than this. Paul's first letter to the Thessalonians is regarded by many scholars as his earliest, and if so, it would be the earliest of all the writings which eventually came to form the New Testament. It is dated variously between AD 41 and 51 – that is, within ten or twenty years of the crucifixion. In it Paul talks about Jesus in remarkable ways, with the obvious assumption that the Christians in Thessalonica already accepted and agreed with what he says (that is, it was already part of the worship and teaching of the church). He speaks of 'the Lord Jesus Christ' in the same breath as 'God the Father' (1:1,3). He can even address prayer to both together (3:11-13). Jesus is 'God's Son', who will come to bring in the final act of judgement and salvation (1:10). In the Old Testament, that last great final day was described as 'the Day of the LORD [Yahweh]' (e.g. Joel 1:15; 2:11, 28-32; 3:14 etc). The expected coming of Jesus has transformed it into the Day of the Lord Jesus (1 Thess 4:16 - 5:2). And Jesus is our salvation in that day because he both died and rose again (1:10; 4:14) in order to save us from that judgement (1:10; 5:9).

We can get just too familiar with this kind of language in the letters of Paul and other New Testament documents, with the result that we do not see how astounding it is. Such was the impact of Jesus, such was the power of the memory of his amazing life and words, such was *Such was the impact of Jesus* the experienced reality of his risen presence and power, that almost immediately (as Acts shows, which, though written later than 1 Thessalonians, of course, describes the earliest followers of Jesus in Jerusalem immediately after the resurrection) he was being exalted, worshipped, prayed to and talked about alongside the one true living God of the Jewish Scriptures.

I am stressing this because there is still a widely-held popular view that the New Testament itself makes no claims about the deity of Jesus. It was only centuries later that the church, under the influence of Greek philosophy, came to regard him as divine and formulated a 'Christology' of incarnation. We are asked to imagine a simple, homely Jesus, somewhat embellished by Paul, and only deified in the later legends of the church. Unfortunately this caricature of historical reality (for that is frankly what it is) receives some of its credibility from the work of certain schools of biblical scholarship. But there is simply masses of evidence to show that it will not stand up as a truthful account of the early years of the movement which emerged from those who first witnessed Jesus of Nazareth. Fortunately also there are many good books available to help us think more clearly and more accurately on this matter.[9]

Conclusion

What we have seen in this chapter is, first, that the Bible presents us with a radical and comprehensive understanding of the sinful predicament of the human race. It thus prepares us to appreciate what salvation has to be and that only God can save us. In the face of such depth, to talk of Jesus as merely one among any number of 'saving points of contact with God' seems an altogether trivial account of his significance.

Second, the Old Testament portrays God's saving intention and action in and through his people Israel as something unique. The Messiah, therefore, as the one who embodied Israel, embodied also their uniqueness.

Third, we saw that the Old Testament throbs with the growing expectation and desire that God himself would come bringing salvation. The impact of Jesus was such that those who encountered him came to realise not merely that the Messiah had indeed come, but also that in Jesus of Nazareth they had encountered Yahweh, the God of Israel, himself. So powerful was this realisation that, incredibly for monotheistic Jews, they could take the step of applying to Jesus Scriptures that had referred to Yahweh. And they did this, not merely in the 'love language' of hymns like Philippians 2, but in sober theological argument, such as in Hebrews 1.

In Jesus, then, the uniqueness of Israel and the uniqueness of Yahweh flow together for he embodied the one and he incarnated the other. So he shares and fulfils the identity and the mission of both.

In conclusion, however, we need to remember that the truth of Isaiah 45:23 (that all nations will acknowledge Yahweh as God and Saviour), as well as its application to Jesus in Philippians 2:5-11, lies in our future hope. That is to say, we still look forward to it being demonstrated to all nations and accepted by them. Yes, we have the historical facts and the witness of the Old Testament and its fulfilment and endorsement in the New Testament. But our claim that Jesus of Nazareth was Yahweh in human flesh, that he is exalted as Lord, that he is unique as God's final act of revelation and salvation – all these remain the affirmation of faith. A faith which, for us who know him and the power of God through him, amounts to certainty and total conviction. But also a hope – in the biblical sense of confident expectation – that the truth we now perceive by faith will be finally and conclusively demonstrated. And the responsibility for that final demonstration and proof rests not with us but with God. For we, like Israel, are simply witnesses in the case. 'You are my witnesses,' said Yahweh to Israel (Is 43:10). 'You will be my witnesses,' echoed Jesus to his disciples, '... to the ends of the earth' (Acts 1:8). The uniqueness of Jesus is not something Christianity invented. It is a truth which has been entrusted to us as stewards and witnesses. The final proof of it rests with God himself who, meanwhile, has exalted him to the highest place and given him his own supreme name.

6

The Bible and Human Religions

In the last chapter we looked at how the Bible shapes our understanding of the uniqueness of Jesus, especially in the light of his own Scriptures – the Old Testament. But what light does the Bible shed on the religions of the world as such? In this chapter we shall survey some key themes, in the order in which they occur in the Bible, which contribute to a biblical understanding of religions.

The Bible and Human Religions

The first thing we have to say here may come as something of a surprise, and that is that 'religion' is not really a biblical word at all.[1] You won't find it very often in the Bible, and you can check a concordance if you don't believe me! The Bible is concerned, not with religious systems as such, but with people and their lives on earth before God. People may worship false gods, but the Bible does not give much attention to the religious content of their belief and practice. Even the religion of the people of God, as a mixture of human response and divine revelation, seems to be as much the target of criticism and rebuke as anything else. Labels are not what matter. God looks on the heart, and the prophets looked at behaviour, and neither were fooled or dazzled by the claims or clutter of religious activity.

Creation and Fall

The creation narratives in Genesis 1-3 present us with humanity as a whole, represented in and by Adam (the generic name for the human race as well as the name of the first man), made in the image of God and placed in *In God's image* the midst of the earth, there to live before God our Creator. The whole human race, therefore, has the capacity of being addressed by God and of making response to God. That indeed is the very essence of what it means to be human, in God's image. We are the creatures who know of our origin from God, and are aware of our accountability to God. At this point in the Bible story there is no question of 'religion' or 'religions' as some separate dimension of life. It makes no sense to ask the question, for example, 'What religion were Adam and Eve?' Human beings respond to God in the totality of their life within God's creation. God 'walks and talks' with them. Human life is God-conscious and God-related in every dimension of our existence.

The Dutch theologian, J. Blauw, put it like this:

> A man without 'religion' is a contradiction in itself. In his 'religion' man gives account of his relation to God. His religion is reaction upon the (real or pretended) revelation of God. Man is 'incurably religious' because his relation to God belongs to the very essence of man himself. Man is only man as man before God.[2]

But the same Genesis narratives also present us with the fact of humanity fallen and living in rebellion against God. Adam and

In rebellion   Eve, after their disobedience, try to hide from God. Cain goes away from the presence of God after attempting to evade his responsibility to God for his brother. So the whole human race lives in a state of flight from God – hiding from the very God on whom we depend for life and breath, and to whom we are inescapably answerable for all our actions.

This divided, dual nature of human existence is a fundamental point in thinking clearly about human beings and religion. On the one hand, as the image of God, we still reflect our Creator, respond to him, recognise his hand in creation and, along with the rest of the animal creation, look to the hand of God for the very supports of life itself (Ps 104:27ff). God is involved in the whole of life, for we are human only through our relationship with God. We cannot therefore utterly remove God from ourselves without ceasing to be human. This fact about humanity is prior to any specific, distinctively 'religious' belief or practice. Our fellow human being is first, foremost and essentially a person made in the image of God, and only secondarily a Hindu, Muslim or secular pagan. So, inasmuch as their religion is part of their humanity, whenever we meet people whom we call 'adherents of another religion', we meet people who, in their religion as in all else, have *some* relationship to the Creator God. We might add to this that all human beings also live in a form of covenant relationship to God as the preserver of life on earth, through the commitment he made in the covenant with Noah (Gen 8:21 – 9:17). Whatever a person's religion, he or she lives in God's earth as the beneficiary of God's providential faithfulness, in spite of the horrors of human depredation of the planet and inhumanity to each other.

Nevertheless, on the other hand, we have to add at once that this relationship has been corrupted by sin so that in religion, again as in all else, people live in a state of rebellion and disobedience against the living God. Indeed, if religion is 'man giving account of his relation to God', it will be in the religious dimension of human life that we would expect to find the clearest evidence of the radical fracture of that relationship. If the immediate response of the fallen Adam in us is to hide from the presence of the living God, what more effective way could there be than through religious activity which gives us the illusion of having met and satisfied him? Religious observance can in fact be a form of subtle escape from the God we are afraid and ashamed to meet for real. The fallen duplicity of humanity is that we *simultaneously* seek after God our Maker and flee from God our Judge. Human religions, therefore, simultaneously manifest both these human tendencies because they express both sides of our human nature.

Now when we put together both sides of the last two paragraphs, it means that we have to avoid sweeping generalisations about religions – saying either that they are all evil and satanic, or that they are all good and helpful. Neither is entirely true, because human beings themselves are neither wholly evil nor wholly good. *Are religions good or bad?* Human religions show all the marks of human ambiguity. Since the Bible affirms that all human beings are made in God's image and are related in some way to God as Creator, it is an unbiblical exaggeration to assign all non-Christian religious faith and life to the work of the devil. Nevertheless it is equally unbiblical to overlook the realm of the satanic and the demonic in human religions – often (as Jesus discovered) most subtly at its strongest in what appears as 'the best' in them.

The patriarchs

As we saw above in Chapter 5, the story of God's redemptive work in history begins in Genesis 12 with the call of Abraham and the covenant with him and his descendants. But the stage and scenery are set in Genesis 10 and 11, which describe the world of nations. These are 'the nations' whose idols and rites will later be condemned or mocked by the prophets and psalmists. They are also 'the nations' who, as enemies of Israel, will threaten and harass God's redeemed people, and who will repeatedly be placed at the sharp end of God's words and deeds of judgement. Yet it is precisely for the sake of these nations that Abraham was called and Israel was chosen. In the covenant with Abraham, Israel is chosen *among* the nations *for* the nations, so that 'all peoples on earth will be blessed' (Gen 12:3).

Among the nations, for the nations

> Here it becomes clear that the whole history of Israel is nothing but the continuation of God's dealings with the nations, and that therefore the history of Israel is only to be understood from the unsolved problem of the relation of God to the nations.[3]

God's election of Israel, therefore, does not imply the rejection of the rest of humanity. Rather it is set in close context with the prospect and promise of blessing for the nations through Israel. This is a vital point to bear in mind when we come to observe the religious exclusivism of later, Mosaic and post-Mosaic, Old Testament faith. Israel was commanded to reject the gods and religions of the other nations. But that did not at all mean that those nations were themselves rejected from God's saving purpose. On the contrary, Israel was chosen for their sake.

There is a marked difference between the religious faith and practice of the ancestors of Israel in Genesis and the developed system of worship of Israel after the Exodus and Sinai covenant. The most obvious contrast lies in the use of *Patriarchal* divine names. The patriarchs worshipped the *religion* Mesopotamian and west Semitic high god, El, sometimes with a variety of other additional names.[4] They receive commands and promises from him directly (without prophets) and they build altars and offer sacrifices to him (without priests). Their relationship to El is one of obedience and trust and is described as a covenant which included promises of divine protection and the provision of land and children (especially Gen 15:17-18).

Now the writer of Genesis clearly identifies El as he is known and responded to by the patriarchs with Yahweh, the personal name of Israel's redeeming, covenant God. *El and* However, study of the use of divine names in Genesis *Yahweh* shows that the writer makes this identification in a carefully controlled way. Normally it is in the narrative sections that the author uses the name Yahweh on its own when referring to God. Since he is telling the story from the standpoint of his own faith presuppositions, he and his readers know that the God they are talking about, the God who called Abraham and whom Abraham believed and obeyed, was in fact the God Yahweh. But in the dialogue sections, particularly where God is the speaker, either the old El-title of God is used on its own, or Yahweh is added alongside an El-title. It appears that while the author wished to indicate that it was indeed Yahweh who addressed the patriarchs, and to whom they responded, he did not wish to violate or suppress the ancient traditions by obscuring the names by which they had in fact worshipped God. He knew that the ancestors of Israel used El names for God; but he also knew that that God was later known as Yahweh, and so he could use that name too when telling the story for his contemporary readers.

This fits with God's words to Moses in Exodus 6:3 concerning the contrast between the revelation of the name Yahweh now being made to Moses on the one hand, and the patriarchs' knowledge of him as El Shaddai on the other. 'I appeared to Abraham, to Isaac and to Jacob as God Almighty [El Shaddai], but by my name the LORD [Yahweh] I did not make myself known to them.' The most natural interpretation of this text is that the *name* Yahweh was not known to the patriarchs, though the *God* Yahweh was. The editor of the Pentateuch evidently saw no contradiction between such an assertion in Exodus and the Genesis viewpoint that Yahweh, God of Israel, was in fact the prime mover of the patriarchal history.

What we have here is a situation where the living God was known, worshipped, believed and obeyed, but under divine titles

The living God and local gods
which were common to the rest of contemporary semitic culture, and some of which at least, according to some scholars, may originally have belonged to separate deities or localisations of El. This raises a question which is relevant to the matter of what status we give to the names of gods in other religions today. Can we infer from the Genesis stories that people today may actually worship and relate personally to the true, living God, but do so under the name or names of some 'local' deity known to them in their own religion, without knowledge of God's saving name and action in Christ?[5]

To answer this question we need to note carefully the special and particular nature of God's relationship with the patriarchs. The fact that the living God addressed Abraham and entered into covenant with him in terms of divine names that Abraham would already have known, in no way implies that all Abraham's contemporaries who worshipped El using those names, and with the more sordid side of the mythology associated with El, thereby knew and worshipped the living God. It does not even imply that Abraham's own religious belief and practice constituted worship of the living God, or was acceptable to God before the point where God addressed him and he responded in obedient faith. The relationship between God and Abraham was based on God's initiative in grace and self-revelation, not on the name of the deity Abraham already knew, by itself, nor on the quality or sincerity of Abraham's previous worship (about which we are told nothing anyway). And the reason why God revealed himself to Abraham was not to give approval to the religion of El and all the gods associated with him, but to lead Abraham and his descendants beyond it into a personal, covenant relationship with God. Through faith and obedience, Abraham and his descendants would come to a fuller experience of redemption and thereby to a fuller knowledge of the living God's true name and character.[6]

So the patriarchal experience certainly allows us to believe that God does address and relate to people in terms of their existing concept of deity (as in the case of Cornelius). But we must presume that such initiative is preparatory to bringing them to a knowledge of his historic revelation and redemptive acts (which, in our era, means knowledge of Christ). It does not allow us to assert that all worship of other gods is in itself unconscious worship of the true God, nor to escape from the task of bringing knowledge of the saving name and work of God in Jesus Christ to people of other faiths.

A final point on the patriarchs arises from the brief reference to them in Joshua 24:14f. Joshua, seeking to renew the covenant and having recounted the mighty redemptive acts of Yahweh, challenges the people to get rid *Choose whom you will serve* of all other gods, and serve Yahweh alone in accordance with the covenant. Among the examples of such 'other gods', Joshua cites not only the gods of Canaan and Egypt, but 'the gods your forefathers (i.e. Abraham, etc.) worshipped beyond the River'. What this means is that although God initially accommodated his relationship with the patriarchs to their previous worship and concepts of deity (as was necessary in the period historically prior to the Exodus), now that their descendants have a much clearer knowledge of Yahweh in the light of the Exodus, Sinai and the conquest, such previous concepts are inadequate and indeed cannot fit in with covenant loyalty to Yahweh alone. This text shows how difficult it was in practice for Israel to live in the midst of polytheism and idolatry, when their own roots lay in the polytheism of Mesopotamia. But the answer to the difficulty was not a tolerant syncretism that accepted all the old gods. Rather they were called to a radical rejection of all other gods apart from the God known to them as Yahweh through his acts of revelation and redemption up to that point in history. How much more is this the case for us who stand on 'this side' of the completion of God's revelation and redemption in Jesus Christ?

Israel and the gods of the nations in the Old Testament

There is certainly a change of atmosphere from the apparent friendly neutrality of the patriarchs towards the religion of their

No other gods Canaanite neighbours in Genesis, to the clarity and unambiguous exclusiveness of the first commandment: 'I am the LORD [Yahweh]... You shall have no other gods before me' (Ex. 20:2-3). From this point on, the faith of Israel was dogmatically mono-Yahwistic, whether or not all the *monotheistic* implications of that faith were as yet consciously understood. Israel was forbidden either to worship other gods or to attempt to worship Yahweh in the way those other gods were worshipped (Deut 12:30f). In the Law (e.g. Deut 7, 13 etc), in the prophets (e.g. Jer 2), in the narratives (e.g. 2 Kings 17), in the Psalms (e.g. Ps 106), even in the Wisdom tradition (e.g. Job 31:26ff), the overwhelming message is of the exclusiveness of Israel's faith – Yahweh alone. This is not just a peripheral trait or the by-product of national pride. It is of the very essence of Israel's covenant relationship with God.

However, it is precisely as we feel the full force of this particularism and exclusivism of the historical faith of Israel in the Old Testament that we need to recall the universal purpose

For the sake which lay behind it. The preservation of the worship *of the nations* of the living God in Israel and of the revelation entrusted to them was not to spite the rest of humanity, but was ultimately for their sake. It was not a matter of Israel flaunting their privilege in an attitude of 'Our religion is better than yours' – as if Israel's religion was a superior brand on the supermarket shelf. Rather, what was at stake, and what was so threatened by Israel compromising with the gods and worship of other nations, was the continuance of the redemptive work of the Creator God for all humanity.

God chose to entrust the experience and knowledge of his salvation to the unique historical and social context of Israel. But that was nothing to be proud of. It was certainly not due to any national or religious superiority on Israel's part, as they were bluntly informed (cf. Deut 7:7; 9:5f). On the contrary, it was in spite of their weakness and failure that Israel received the mission of being a holy (distinctive) and priestly (representing God) nation (Ex 19:3-6). In the light of such a responsibility, for Israel to have accepted Canaanite and other religions as equally valid and acceptable alternatives to their own faith would not have been an act of tolerance, kindness or maturity. It would have been an utter betrayal of the rest of mankind, for the sake of whose salvation they had been chosen and redeemed.

The social effects of religion

We need to remember that religions are not just systems of beliefs and concepts. They are also part of total world-views and are integrally related to the social, economic and often political structures of life of their followers. This was as true in the ancient world as it is today. The difference between Israel and the Canaanites and other surrounding societies was not a simple difference over what gods were to be worshipped and how many they might be. Israel was distinctive in her total social system from both the Canaanite system she replaced, and other contemporary ancient Near Eastern cultures. And that social distinctiveness was an integral part of how Israel understood her religion and its requirements. She was meant to be different – visibly, socially, practically, different – from the surrounding nations.[7]

Elijah's encounter with Ahab after the murder of Naboth in 1 Kings 21 illustrates this point very clearly. Jezebel's treatment of Naboth and his family was not just to satisfy Ahab's greed. It was an act of socio-cultural imperialism based on Jezebel's concept of political power (where the monarch could do as he pleased with the land and subjects he virtually owned), and her concept of economic practice (where land was a commercial commodity, not an inalienable family trust). In both respects her cultural background was diametrically opposed to Israel's social system. And the Baal religious cult she championed was an integral part of her social and political views.

Yahweh or Baal?

The struggle between Yahweh and Baal for the soul of Israel was not merely 'religious', but thoroughly social; not just a question of who was the true God (as on Mt Carmel), but of

Justice or oppression?

how Israelites were to live and treat each other. The religion of
Jezebel sanctioned and sanctified a system of politics, economics
and social life which was autocratic, oppressive and exploitative.
Baalism was the religious ethos of that kind of society, the unjust
social outworking of fallen, idolatrous humanity, the native soil
and element of a Jezebel. Israel's relationship to Yahweh, in clear
and deliberate contrast, demanded and had originally created a
social system based on liberty (in the comprehensive deliverance
of the Exodus), equality (in the economic division of the land)
and fraternity (even the king was 'one of your brothers', Deut
17:15, 20). Such words sound revolutionary! And indeed Israel
was revolutionary, when compared with her contemporaries, both
in religious and social life.

> To worship Yahweh, to be an Israelite, meant... to practise a specific
> way of life in separation from and in overt opposition to time-
> honoured established ways of life regarded throughout the ancient
> Near East as inevitable if not totally desirable.[8]

It is vital that we remember this integration of spiritual and social
realities when assessing other religions. We must avoid the idea
that religion is something for *God's* good, as if we ought to choose
the right God because he will be piqued if we don't. God's
revelation and the response it demands are for *humanity's* own
good. To choose the true God is to opt for the truly human as well.
Conversely, idolatry and injustice still go together as much today
as in ninth-century Samaria. Some of the most deeply ingrained
social oppressions in our world are integrally linked to religions
which sanction them.

Prophetic satire against false gods

A prominent feature of the account of the great conflict between
Yahweh and Baal on Mt Carmel is Elijah's mockery of the
prophets of Baal for the manifest impotence of their god (1 Kings
18:27-29). This satire against other gods is found also in Isaiah
44:9-20 and we need to comment on both texts.

In 1 Kings 18:27-29, we may make two comments on Elijah's
scorn. First of all, it was directed, not at the mass of the people,

but at the false prophets. The people were like witnesses to a case who were challenged to make a clear verdict (v 21). The mockery was on those who had led the people astray from their God and were in *Not mockery of sincere followers* fact responsible for the judgement of drought they were suffering. In this respect it is comparable to Jesus' own sarcasm against the Pharisees and religious leaders who were actually keeping people out of the kingdom of God. Second, this was not mockery of sincere followers of other religions. These were men who had once belonged to God's own people but had turned aside and rejected Yahweh, his covenant and its demands. Apart from Jezebel's own imported prophets of Baal and Asherah, the Israelites among Elijah's opponents were apostates from the faith of Yahweh, not the unenlightened followers of some other religion.

In Isaiah 44:9-20, it is the idolater himself, the worshipper of other gods, who attracts the prophet's satire. This passage is preceded by earlier comments on the futility and contemptible impotence of idols (cf. Is 40:19f; 41:7, 21ff, etc). Those earlier passages referred to the great state gods of Babylon and asserted that Yahweh is incomparably superior to them – an important pastoral/evangelistic point for those the prophet was preparing for release and return from Babylonian captivity. But here the butt is home-made idolatry, which is practically the domestic by-product of eating and heating. Again two brief comments.

First, the prophet recognises that such idol worshippers are to some degree blinded, deluded and misled (vv 9, 18, 20). Idolatry is not stupidity, but involves a blindness which is partly wilful and culpable and partly the work of some external force or power. There are links here with Paul's teaching in Romans 1:21-25 and 2 Corinthians 4:4.

Second, sometimes scholars criticise the Old Testament prophets on the grounds that they did not understand the inner dynamic of idol-worship. They did not realise, it is alleged, that there was a distinction between the physical idol and the spirit, or deity that was symbolised or localised in the idol. But this criticism is invalid. What aroused the prophet's scornful wonder was the sight of any living human being bowing in worship to

something other than the one incomparable living God (vv 6-8) –
regardless of whether that 'something' was the idol itself or the
deity it represented. Furthermore, the prophet was, in fact, well
aware of the difference between a material idol and the deity it
supposedly figured. He knew that the worshippers thought of the
actual deity being 'in heaven', not identical with the statue itself.
For in Isaiah 46:1f he pictured Bel and Nebo, two of the most
prominent and powerful Babylonian gods, looking down from
'heaven' and watching their statues being carried away by their
worshippers on earth in defeat and disgrace. Such is the
impotence of these *gods* that they cannot save their own *idols,* let
alone save their worshippers!

In any case, the prophet's purpose here and in all these
passages was not to describe the psychology of idolatry, but to
contrast it devastatingly with the proven reality and power of
Yahweh, the living God. He was not the neutral chairman of a
polite dialogue between the religions of Israel and Babylon, but
the proclaimer of the imminent victory of the Lord of the universe
and history, beside whom all other claimants to deity were indeed
contemptible.

> The whole Old Testament (and the New Testament as well) is filled
> with descriptions of how Yahweh-Adonai, the covenant God of Israel,
> is waging war against those forces which try to thwart and subvert his
> plans for his creation. He battles against those false gods which
> human beings have fashioned from the created world, idolised, and
> used for their own purpose... the Baals and the Ashteroth, whose
> worshippers elevated nature, the tribe, the state and the nation to a
> divine status. God fights against magic and idolatry which, according
> to Deuteronomy, bend the line between God and his creation. He
> contends against every form of social injustice and pulls off every
> cloak under which it seeks to hide.[9]

The goal of this prolonged struggle was that ultimately not only
Israel but every nation of humanity will acknowledge
that Yahweh, God of Israel, is in reality the only true
and living God of all the earth. This is not portrayed
as a struggle of religions as such. It is simply taken for granted, in
a sense, as an implication of Israel's monotheism. That is to say,

*A vision for
the future*

if indeed Yahweh is God and there is no other (Deut 4:35,39), then the day must come when that will be recognised by all humanity. In the texts that envisage this, it is notable that it is not framed in terms of Israel's religion, but of Israel's God. Isaiah 45:14, 23-24, for example, portray the nations saying *not*, 'Now we know that your religion was best,' but 'Now we know that Yahweh truly is God' (cf. Is 60:6, 9). Similarly, Philippians 2 emphasises that everyone will ultimately acknowledge that Jesus is Lord, not, gloatingly, that Christians were right all along. This recognition is generally expressed in terms of joy and celebration among the nations, especially in the Psalms (cf. Pss 47, 96-98), but also in the prophets (cf. Is 2:2-5; 19:19-25; 45:22-25; Amos 9:11f).

Perhaps this is the best context in which to comment on Malachi 1:11 – often referred to by broader inclusivists as a text which seems to support the view that the worship of people of other religions is pleasing and acceptable to God. It is thus used as a proof text for a more universalistic approach to other religions.

To this interpretation one has to say, first, that the text does not speak of other *religions,* but of the name of Yahweh being great among the *nations.* Since Malachi and his hearers knew full well that the *God's name among the nations* nations did not in literal fact worship the name of Yahweh, the meaning of his words is more likely to be found in a non-literal interpretation, as we shall see.

Second, the tense of the verse is not explicit. In the Hebrew text of the verse there is no finite verb, so the words can be translated in either a present or a future sense ('great *is* my name', or 'great *will be* my name'). Some commentators, and the NIV, take it in the latter sense as an eschatological vision of the nations in the future bringing acceptable worship to Yahweh.

> My name will be great among the nations, from the rising to the setting of the sun. In every place incense and pure offerings will be brought to my name, because my name will be great among the nations.

However, this translation, though grammatically possible, seems to spoil the point of the *contrast* Malachi is making between the unacceptable present worship of the Israelite priesthood and the worship of the nations. That is, it makes little sense to say 'You are not worshipping me acceptably now; but some day the nations will bring me acceptable worship.'

So, third, it seems more likely that Malachi is speaking in a highly ironic, or sarcastic fashion. He is vigorously accusing Israel for profaning the true worship of Yahweh with diseased and inadequate offerings and saying that even the worship of the pagan nations is more acceptable to God in comparison. This verse would then be a rhetorical, ironic comparison intended rather to shame Israel than soberly to describe pagan nations or approve their worship. A similar rhetorical technique occurs in Ezekiel 16:49-52 where Israel and Judah are compared with Sodom and Gomorrah, who are then said to be *righteous* in comparison with Israel's wickedness! The whole section Malachi 1:7-14 is a condemnation of Israel, and verse 11 is in that context and should not be taken in isolation as an independent approving comment on the nations.[10]

God leading the nations? Another text sometimes misused to suggest that all peoples are already related redemptively to God is Amos 9:7: 'Are not you Israelites the same to me as the Cushites?' declares the Lord. 'Did I not bring Israel up from Egypt, the Philistines from Caphtor and the Arameans from Kir?' But again we have to observe that this verse also, in its context, is not so much a statement about the other nations as a severe indictment of Israel. It makes the point that Israel had no special claim on God's favour just because of their historical Exodus on its own. At the level of human history and geography, God had been active and sovereign in the movements and migrations of other nations too. What the verse is saying is that the Israelites, by their blatant social disobedience and injustice had become no better in God's sight than any nation as foreign or as far away as they could think of (Cushites were Ethiopians). It does not say that these other nations were in the same relation to God as Israel were, or that they were already in any sense the people of God. Amos had already affirmed quite the opposite of such a view in

Amos 3:2. He is not saying that the nations were like Israel, but that Israel had become like the nations in God's sight through their wickedness, and they needn't think that the mere fact of the Exodus gave them some kind of immunity from his judgement. In other words, Amos 9:7 is a challenge to complacency among God's people; it is not a direct statement about the redeemed status of any other people.

Jesus and the kingdom of God in the New Testament

When we turn to the New Testament, we see that Jesus came proclaiming the kingdom of God. He was not talking about a place or realm, but about a 'state of affairs' – the dynamic, active reign of God among human beings, which was breaking into history in a new way with Jesus' own arrival and which demanded urgent response. Our understanding of what Jesus meant by the phrase 'the kingdom of God' must start from the fact that he was proclaiming the fulfilment of Jewish hopes springing out of the Old Testament ('the time is fulfilled...'). And in the Old Testament the kingship of God has at least three layers of meaning.[11]

i) God reigns as universal sovereign over the whole earth (e.g. 2 Kings 19:15; Pss 99, 145, etc). Nothing takes place beyond his providence or outside his control. The affairs of nations in history are under his universal reign – both in general terms (eg Prov 21:1) and specifically as they relate to his own people, whether God uses other nations in punishment on Israel (e.g. Is 8:6-10; 10:5-6), or for their deliverance (e.g. Is 45). The very first declaration in the Bible that 'Yahweh reigns' has this universal sovereignty in view, for it celebrates his victory over the opposing power of Pharaoh, in the Song of Moses (Ex 15:18).

ii) God was acknowledged as king specifically within Israel, because of the unique covenant relationship between them. God's kingship is related to his protection (Num 23:21-23), and to his giving of the law (Deut 33:3-5) – both of which were primary duties of kings for their subjects. It was, for several centuries, the reason why Israel had no human king (Judg 8:23). And the kingship of God over Israel was to be expressed and 'earthed' through social justice (Pss 97:2; 99:4; 146:7-10).

iii) But it was obvious in the Old Testament, on the one hand that the nations of the world did not yet acknowledge the universal rule of Yahweh as king (sense i), and, on the other hand, that even in Israel his kingship (sense ii) was not obeyed in reality in the life of the nation. And so there developed an eschatological, future dimension to the theme – that is, a future hope that God would some day intervene to establish his reign in its fullness, over Israel, the nations, and the world. God would come as king and put things right. A number of prophetic passages include this idea (e.g. Jer 23:1-6; Ezek 34; Is 52:7-10; Mic 4:2-8; Zech 9:9-10), and it was anticipated with joyful expectation in Israel's worship (e.g. Ps 98: 4-9).

The future now   The kingdom of God *as proclaimed by Jesus* relates primarily to the third dimension. What the people were expecting as something in the future, Jesus proclaimed, has now come among them in the present. 'The kingdom of God *is at hand*!' His own coming had inaugurated the final great arrival of the reign of God – even though in surprising and initially hidden ways, as his parables made clear. And the climax of that coming of the kingdom of God was the climax of the Gospels themselves – i.e. the great events of the death and resurrection of Jesus, in which God's reign decisively overthrew the power of sin and death.

Is the kingdom of God 'at work in other religions'?

This specific sense of Jesus' proclamation of the kingdom of God means that we have to be very careful in 'thinking clearly' about the expression that 'the kingdom of God is at work in other religions', which one sometimes hears or reads in the inter-faith discussion. It is a very slippery concept, and those who use it sometimes mean quite different things. For example:

Is the phrase intended to mean that God *is sovereignly at work among all human beings*, regardless of their religion, working out his purpose in all human history as the Lord of history and nature (i.e. the first dimension)? If this is what is meant, then it is undoubtedly a biblical truth, but it is hardly what Jesus meant by his proclamation of the kingdom of God. He announced something which was taking effect in a radical new way with his own arrival. But that was certainly not the case as regards God's providential sovereignty.

The universal kingship of God has been at work in the world since creation; it did not 'arrive' with the coming of Jesus. Also, the kingdom of God as taught by Jesus in ***Seed or yeast*** his parables was something which, from small beginnings in his own ministry, would grow and spread like seed or yeast. Again, God's universal sovereignty can hardly be said to 'grow' in that way. And thirdly, entering or belonging to the kingdom of God is virtually identical, according to Jesus, with faith, obedience and discipleship to Jesus himself. But the first dimension of God's kingship does not depend on such faith and discipleship. God reigns over the history of people and nations with or without their obedience, co-operation, or even their conscious knowledge (witness Pharaoh, Nebuchadnezzar, Cyrus, for example). Most significantly, the Jewish opponents of Jesus, even when they rejected and crucified him, were carrying out the sovereign purpose of God. They were subject in that respect to the first dimension of his kingship (Acts 2:23). But through their persistence in unbelief they remained outside the kingdom of God as taught, brought and embodied by Jesus himself.

Is the phrase then intended to mean that *the kingdom of God is at work redemptively within other religions* (i.e. that other religions are the arena of God's kingship in a way similar to its second dimension in Israel)? Certainly we will want to say (as we already have), that God works within the hearts and environments of people before they come to personal knowledge of Jesus and to repentance, faith and obedience in relation to him. In that sense, yes, God can be at work within the context of other religions. The Bible includes the stories of people in whose lives God worked who came from outside the people of God originally, ***God is*** but came to acknowledge the living God (e.g. Naaman, ***ahead of us*** the widow of Zarephath, Nebuchadnezzar, Cornelius). But our awareness of such divine presence and activity in the world beyond the boundaries of the church ought to be an incentive to evangelism – i.e. taking the saving knowledge of the name of Jesus to those he is already preparing to receive it.

It is one of the great encouragements of mission to know that God is ahead of us already by his Spirit preparing the hearts of those who have not yet heard, to receive the gospel gladly when they do hear (cf. Acts 16:14).

But if the phrase in this sense is intended to mean that God saves people *by means of other religions*, then this is open to the objections we discussed in Chapter 3, on inclusivism. Unfortunately, some of those who affirm that 'the kingdom of God is at work among other religions', rather than taking that as an incentive for evangelism, take it to mean that evangelism is unnecessary, and even offensive. If God is saving people through the operation of his kingdom in other religions, then what need have we to try to make them Christians? Indeed, on this view, evangelism is regarded as quite inappropriate. We should rather encourage them to be better followers of their own religion (a view that is seriously argued by some).

In my view, the most telling contradiction of this view that the presence of the kingdom of God somehow neutralises the need for evangelism in Jesus' name, is the experience of Jesus himself among his own contemporaries. Here were a people privileged beyond all other peoples with the knowledge of God and his mighty acts, a people who knew the meaning of the kingship of Yahweh in their covenant relationship, a people who were actually and passionately awaiting the kingdom of God. Yet when it came among them in the very person of Jesus and in amazing demonstration of its power before their very eyes, many of them still refused to enter or were very slow to. Here surely is proof that the mere *presence* of the kingdom of God among a people or in a situation in no way guarantees that all those who witness it can be counted among the redeemed, or be thought to be beyond the need of the explicit evangelistic challenge of faith and obedience towards Jesus Christ. The command and prophecy of Jesus must still hold priority, that 'this gospel of the kingdom will be preached in the whole world as a testimony to all nations' (Mt 24:14).

The prologue of John's Gospel

The prologue of John's Gospel, along with other passages where the cosmic nature and work of Christ are referred to (such as Col 1:15ff; Heb 1:1ff), is clearly very important in any discussion of the relation between Christ and other faiths. There are two very important words in it which are relevant to this issue:

1. *Light.* 'The true light that gives light to every man was coming into the world' (Jn 1:9). This seems to me the correct rendering of the ambiguous Greek of this verse.[12] The preceding context tells us of John the Baptist's role as herald of the light. At that point Christ, who enlightens all human beings continuously, was 'on his way', so to speak, into that particular historical span of space and time which he would occupy in the world.

What is meant by this 'enlightening' of all? It is urged by some that if all people receive light from the cosmic Christ, then all are in some saving relationship with God through him – whether conscious of it or not. This Christ-light is already there in all humans. In evangelism, therefore, if it be allowed at all, we do not take Christ to people of other religions, but we meet the Christ already in them through the light he has already shed in them.

All enlightened – all saved?

However, this flies in the face of the immediate context and the rest of the gospel. If the enlightening of all humanity in verse 9 means that all already have *saving* knowledge of God, then what was the necessity or purpose of the light becoming incarnate? Why the incredible cost of becoming flesh if people are saved by the light they have? And if all human beings are redemptively enlightened by the 'non-incarnate' Christ, why do some reject the light of the incarnate Christ, preferring darkness, and therefore expose themselves to God's judgement (Jn 1:10f; 3:19f)? Consider again Jesus' contemporaries – 'his own'. Here were those who had received more light from the pre-incarnate Christ than any other religious group, through the historical and scriptural revelation we now call the Old Testament. Yet so many of 'his own received him not'. This strongly undermines the idea that it is the 'sincere', the 'devout' or the 'enlightened' – i.e. 'the best' in other religions who are evidence of the presence of this enlightening from Christ in any salvic sense. It was precisely this stratum within Judaism which rejected the incarnate light and crucified him, and, in the person of Saul of Tarsus, went on to persecute his disciples, until the light overpowered Saul to repentance and conversion.

We should not, of course, deny that all moral goodness has its
Not through morality origin in God. (This, you will remember, was one of the points in the inclusivist case that we can accept.) But when this is turned into a redemptive principle, it almost inevitably becomes moralistic, that is, it promises salvation for the best, or at least the better, in a way that is utterly alien to the New Testament. As Lesslie Newbigin puts it:

> It is the 'men of good will', the 'sincere' followers of other religions, the 'observers of the law' who are informed in advance that their seats in heaven are securely booked. This is the exact opposite of the New Testament. Here emphasis is always on surprise. It is the sinner who will be welcomed and those who were confident that their place was secure who will find themselves outside. God will shock the righteous with his limitless generosity and by his tremendous severity.[13]

It is also worth remembering that John is talking here about the enlightenment of *people* as people, *not* about the possibility of light within 'other religions' considered as structural systems of belief, practice and culture. Some commentators use these verses to suggest that the light that shone in Jesus of Nazareth has also shone through other great religious leaders or founders of religious traditions. But the text means nothing of the sort. It is not talking about special light of a religious nature to be found in special people, but about universal light that every human being everywhere shares simply by being human.

The enlightening of verse 9 must surely refer to that knowledge of God which is possessed by every person made in the image of
General revelation God and open to God's general self-revelation. The fact that Christ is said to be the agent of this enlightening does not mean we have to regard it as part of the redemptive work of God in itself. For Christ is part of the unity of the Godhead and shares in the totality of the work of the Godhead, including creation, sustaining of life and revelation (cf Jn 1:3-5; Col 1:15-17; Heb 1:3; 1 Cor 8:6). So the general light of

conscience, moral awareness, and responsibility before God can also be described as light with Christ as its source.

2. *Logos.* The second important word is the one most familiar to us from the famous opening sentence of John's Gospel, 'In the beginning was the Word' – the *logos.* This term is John's way of expressing the truth that Jesus Christ, the incarnate Son of God, was part of the divine reality of God even before the incarnation. The term was already familiar in the world of Greek philosophy, and in that context could mean the great cosmic principle of rationality, order and unity that underlies the whole world of our experience. John's point is that the ultimate, essential, unifying reality of the world is not an abstract principle, but the divine person now known to us through the incarnation of Jesus of Nazareth.

In the early centuries of the church, some Christians worked very hard to understand and defend the Christian faith in relation to the Greek philosophical traditions in which they were educated. Among the most outstanding of these was Justin Martyr, who lived in the mid-2nd century AD. ***Justin Martyr*** He sought to see both the common ground that existed between the great pre-Christian philosophers and the Christian faith, and also the contrasting superiority of the Christian faith to all other philosophies and world-views. Justin asserted that while Plato and other Greek philosophers had not known Jesus, some of them had lived *kata logon*, 'in accordance with the *logos*', and were thereby, in some sense, 'Christians'. In this respect he compared them with Old Testament saints who had not known Jesus either, but lived in the light of the *logos.*

This idea has been taken up in more recent 'Logos theology' and used to imply that other religions are also manifestations in some way of the *logos,* and thus are to ***'Logos theology'*** be accepted as worthy of inclusion in God's saving purpose. However, before looking at one recent example of this way of thinking, it needs to be pointed out that Justin was not simply approving of Greek culture and philosophy in general terms. Rather, he was making the very important discrimination that those philosophers whom he suggested had lived *kata logon* were those who had attacked the idolatry of their own contemporary paganism, such as Socrates. That is, it was not the Greek religion itself that was a manifestation of the *logos,* but on the contrary it was those who saw its inadequacy and rejected its polytheism and its demons who showed evidence of the work of the *logos.*[14] This is not properly acknowledged by those who want to make Justin the patron saint of modern inclusivism.

For example, the Anglican Board of Mission and Unity's report, *Towards a Theology for Inter-Faith Dialogue,*[15] which adopts an inclusivist stance while seeking to maintain the uniqueness of Christ, explains its 'Logos theology' in this way:

> While 'Logos theology' understands the unique expression of God as being in Jesus Christ (there can be no surrendering of that belief), at the same time it takes seriously other manifestations of the *logos* in other places and at other times. This suggests that in relations with those of other faiths, Christians have to hold to that unique self-expressive activity of God in Jesus Christ, safe-guarded and passed down within the Christian church. But equally Christians need to be open to recognise and respond to all manifestations of the *logos*. The decisive revelation of God in Jesus has to be safe-guarded, for that is the canon by which we are enabled to recognise all other manifestations. Furthermore, in the encountering of those other revelations, new depths are discovered in that fullest revelation of God in Jesus Christ. Such reflection on the mystery of the person of Jesus in the Bible and Tradition points in the direction of an inclusivisim in relation to those of other faiths, but with an unswerving loyalty to Jesus Christ.[16]

We can immediately see this as characteristic of the inclusivist position, as described in Chapter 3. It commendably wants to stay *Other manifestations* loyal to Christ and keep him at the centre as the unique and fullest revelation of God. But at the same time it assumes (without argument or supporting biblical evidence) that there have been 'other manifestations of the *logos*'. How then, and for what reasons, is Jesus in fact unique at all, on this understanding? It does seem logically difficult to hold these two ideas together.

Furthermore, this development of 'Logos theology' goes far beyond what John actually says in his prologue, and is virtually incompatible with it. This is what I wrote in criticism of the paragraph quoted above from the BMU report:

> There is so much in this paragraph about 'other manifestations of the Logos in other places and at other times' that a reader might take this as the self-evident gist of John's Logos theme. But it is decidedly not so. Two assertions are made about the universal role of the Logos in John's Prologue. One is his part in the creation of all things and all people. ...The other aspect is that, as Light, the Logos enlightens every human being (v 9). ...Then, against this background of the universal creating and universal enlightening roles of the Logos, John moves on to speak of the one and only actual *manifestation* proper of the Logos – namely the incarnation of the 'one and only' Son of God: 'The Logos became flesh' (v 14). A unique, historical, particular, personally witnessed incarnation is the only mode of 'manifestation of the Logos' to be found in John's Prologue, so unless we are willing to postulate other alleged incarnations as parallels or analogous to Jesus, we should not use John to accredit the idea of 'other manifestations of the Logos' or 'other revelations'. Such ideas are simply not present here.[17]

In other words, it will not do to talk of the *logos* as a kind of cosmic and somewhat abstract 'Christ-principle' which can be alleged to have appeared in other great religious leaders. Inclusivists may like to assert that this has happened, but it is not and cannot be based on any fair interpretation of the meaning of John's words, which tell us that the *logos* 'became flesh' uniquely in Jesus of Nazareth.

Peter and Paul in the book of Acts

The book of Acts is the practical missiology of the early church, written by Luke, a converted Gentile physician who would have had considerable inside knowledge of the gods and religions of the first-century Graeco-Roman world. So it is a book which gives us plenty of material showing how the young Christian faith (even before it was nicknamed 'Christian') confronted the religious environment in which it was born. That environment was really two worlds. There was the world of Jewish faith – the descendant of the Old Testament faith of Israel, though with much additional hopes, practices and traditions in the centuries since the last of the prophets. And there was the world of Greek and Roman religions – many gods, cults, mystical ideas and a whole range of practices, from the official imperial cult of the Roman emperor to the multiplicity of local deities.

The statement of Peter in Acts 4:12 is among the most exclusive texts in the New Testament in affirming the uniqueness of Jesus Christ as the God-given means of salvation: 'Salvation is found in no-one else, for there is no other name under heaven given to men by which we must be saved.' However, there are some who try to avoid the apparent exclusive thrust of the text by pointing on the one hand to the context, which is the healing miracle of Peter, and on the other hand to the Greek in which the same root verb is used for being healed and being saved. Thus, for example, J.V. Taylor says,

No other name

> Peter was saying that Jesus of Nazareth is the source of every act of healing and salvation that has ever happened. He knew perfectly well that vast numbers of people had been healed without any knowledge of Jesus, yet he made the astounding claim that Jesus was the hidden author of all healing. He was the totally unique Saviour because he was totally universal.[18]

Similarly, the BMU report argues,

> The story is about healing and the authority by which this takes place... Peter's reply is not intended to deny the existence of other healings... but to claim that all healing, all making whole, belong to Jesus. It is going beyond the text to interpret it as a statement about other faiths. The context... is not one of comparative religion.[19]

There is a sense in which these statements are right, of course. The context *was* a healing miracle, and Peter was not directly referring to other religions and their salvation claims. However, while it may be 'going beyond the text' to suggest that it addresses the issue of other faiths, it is most certainly falling far short of the text to treat it merely as a statement about healing alone. The story, which spans Acts 3 and 4, includes Peter's powerful evangelistic preaching of the gospel (3:1-26), in which the healing of the cripple is powerful proof of the saving power of Jesus. In that sermon, Peter refers to Jesus as the servant of God (3:13), the 'Holy and Righteous One' (3:14), 'the author of life' (3:15), 'raised from the dead' (3:15), the prophesied Messiah (3:18), the one who would return to bring about the restoration of all things (3:20-21), the fulfilment of the promises to Abraham (3:25), and the one through whom forgiveness of sins could be received by repentance (3:19, 26).

It was because of *these* claims about Jesus (and especially the resurrection), that Peter and John were summoned before the Sanhedrin court (4:2) – *not* just because of 'an act of kindness shown to a cripple' (4:9). So, again, Peter in his statement to the court reaffirms that the healing had taken place in the *Jesus the* name of Jesus (4:10), but immediately goes on from that *expected* undeniable fact (cf. 4:16), to the far greater assertion that *Messiah* Jesus was the expected Messiah and that that was the reason why both salvation and healing were possible through his name. To support this, he used a text already accepted as messianic prophecy (4:11, see Ps 118:22 – also used by Jesus, Mt 21:42-46, and cf. 1 Pet 2:4-10).

So although the text is not explicitly about 'comparative religion', it certainly articulates the conflict between emerging Christianity (which was not yet even called by that name!) and those among the Jewish people who resisted it. And the conflict was precisely over the identity of the Messiah and *The* therefore over the true source of salvation. In the Judaism *source of* of Peter's day, the hope of salvation, in all its wide senses, *salvation* was bound up with the expectation of the coming Messiah. The Messiah alone would bring the fullness of salvation (healing, wholeness, deliverance). The point was that in claiming that Jesus of Nazareth, recently crucified but now witnessed as raised from the dead, was in fact the prophesied Messiah, Peter was also claiming that he alone was the source of salvation. The healing miracle was one among many proofs of the claim, since such healing of the lame was an accepted evidence, as Jesus himself had pointed out to the disciples of John the Baptist (Mt 11:2-6; Lk 7:18-23, quoting Is 35:4-6).

So the text stands as a clear statement of the exclusive nature of salvation as available only through Jesus, as the crucified and risen Messiah. This does not, it seems to me, affect the other question discussed in Chapter 2, concerning the possibility or otherwise of people being saved *by* Christ who never in their lifetime *hear* of Christ. The truth remains: all who will be saved will be saved because of who Jesus of Nazareth is and because of what he has done for us.[20] But it does rule out, in my view, the more inclusivist view that wants to affirm that salvation is to be found in or through other faiths as such, even if that salvation is somehow finally defined or recognised in the light of Christ.

Cornelius

The story of Cornelius is sometimes used by those who want to argue that sincere pagans can be saved apart from knowledge of Christ simply by their fear of God and their good works. The key text used in support of this position is Acts 10:34-35, in which Peter says, 'I now realise how true it is that God does not show favouritism but accepts men from every nation who fear him and do what is right.' To this is added the description of Cornelius as 'devout and God-fearing', righteous, generous to the poor, and regular in prayer to God – all of which had been observed and approved by God himself before Peter was sent to preach Jesus to his family (Acts 10:2-4, 22, 31). Does this then show that Cornelius was already saved before he believed in Jesus?[21]

Again, one has to say that to ask the question that way is somewhat off-beam. First of all, it is clear from the whole context that Peter's statement is not merely a general affirmation that everybody everywhere is saved. It is Peter's recognition (for which he had been prepared by his vision the previous day), that the gospel of Jesus had now broken down the distinction between Jew and Gentile. Whereas previously he had believed that only Jews were acceptable to God as potential candidates for salvation, now he realised that God would accept Gentiles too. That is what he means by God not showing favouritism. If he had

No distinction between Jew and Gentile

meant that people were accepted in the sense of fully saved on the basis of fear of God and doing what is right, then he had no need to go on and preach the story of Christ, the cross and resurrection, and then to speak of 'receiving forgiveness' through faith in him. What Peter meant in 10:34-35 is expressed further in 10:47 – these people too, these Gentiles, had received the Holy Spirit as the obvious sign of repentance and faith, and therefore they too were to be accepted as fully as the *God welcomes* Jewish believers through baptism. If they were *anybody* acceptable to God (10:35; 11:17-18), they must be accepted by the rest of God's people. Peter's point, then, was not that God saves everybody, but that God welcomes anybody.

Secondly, one has to have regard to the unique historical context of the event. In a sense, Cornelius, before his hearing about Jesus, was in the same position as those Gentiles in the Old Testament who came to believe in the living God and act accordingly – like those who are commended for their faith in Hebrews 11, including the pre-Israelites Abel, Enoch and Noah, and the non-Israelite Rahab. So when the question is asked, hypothetically, suppose Cornelius had died while Peter was on his way, would he have been saved? The answer, I believe, is Yes, in the same sense and for the same reason as we regard the Old Testament believers (Israelite and Gentile) as saved through the Christ they never knew, on the basis of God's grace and their obedient, God-fearing faith. Indeed, Cornelius' believing response to God is described in authentically Old Testament terms in 10:4, indicating that that was exactly how he saw himself – one who believed in Yahweh the God of Israel and sought to live according to the pattern of that faith. And he had been personally assured that his prayers were heard and his generosity noted (10:4, 31). Indeed his very existence as a foreigner who sought the God of Israel, rather similarly to the centurion who sought Jesus (Mt 8:5-13; Lk 7:1-10), could be seen as an instance of the answering of Solomon's prayer at the dedication of the temple itself (1 Kings 8:41-43). If Rahab, the widow of Zarephath and Naaman are among the saved, there can be no reason why Cornelius would not have been saved if he had not had his angelic and apostolic visitors, or had died before receiving them.

However, unlike the Old Testament believers, Cornelius lived in the generation in which the Messiah had actually come, and the faith of Israel had reached its fulfilment. Unlike them, he had the opportunity to know Jesus and find the fullness of salvation and redemption for which the Jews were longing when the Messiah would come and redeem Israel (cf. Lk. 2:25-32 [Simeon, like Cornelius, is also described by Luke as 'righteous and devout']; 24:21). That was the message of salvation, much longed for but now a reality, which he would hear from the lips of Peter (11:14).

A key turning point

Cornelius thus becomes a key turning point in the book of Acts in the story of how the gospel went to the Gentiles (though it is preceded by the story of the Ethiopian eunuch in Acts 8:26-40). It is followed by many other occasions when the preaching of Jesus as Messiah and Saviour drew a similar response of welcoming faith from Gentile 'God-fearers' – i.e. non-Jewish adherents to the Jewish faith who seem to have been a kind of devout 'fringe' around the synagogues in Mediterranean cities outside Palestine (cf. Acts. 13:16, 43, 48; 14:1; 16:14, etc). The whole point of the story seems to be: now that Jesus the Messiah has come, salvation must be preached in his name so that people can come through repentance and faith to forgiveness, salvation, eternal life, and the receiving of the Holy Spirit. Cornelius received all these things through hearing the preaching of the gospel of Christ. It is misusing the story to suggest that the favourable comments on Cornelius' 'Old Testament behaviour' before he was evangelised imply that evangelism in general is somehow unnecessary. Certainly God related to him on the level of his current religious experience and commitment. But he still needed to hear the gospel, needed to know about Jesus, needed to have the opportunity to respond in faith, if he was to enter into the joy of salvation, the eschatological blessings of the Holy Spirit, and the baptised community of the messianic Israel of God.

'An unknown God'?

In the very heartland of Greek polytheism, a distressed but courteous Paul confronts the sophisticated and curious Athenians (Acts 17:16-34). Recent scholarly research suggests that Paul was actually summoned before a kind of religious affairs committee of the Athenian authorities which was entitled to scrutinise any attempt to introduce new gods into the city.[22] They would check the credentials of the alleged god, particularly as regards any miracles or favours he was supposed to have done for the city. They would also check the financial ability of the sponsor (whether or not he could afford to build a temple and sustain the religious cult of the new deity). It seemed to the educated people of Athens (17:18) that Paul was in fact seeking to introduce new gods into the city, *New gods in the city* because he was talking about Jesus and Anastasis ('resurrection', which they may have thought was the name of another god). Thus, the words of the Areopagus in 17:19 were not just a polite invitation, but constituted a definite summons for Paul to provide this information so that they could decide whether or not he could be allowed to introduce a new god to the crowded streets of Athens. Their words were perhaps not quite so innocuous as the NIV, 'May we know what this new teaching is that you are presenting', but could be more properly translated: 'We have the authority to make a judgement on what it is being claimed these things are.'

Paul's reply effectively says that the God he is talking about is not one who needs to be served by a temple and a sacrificial cult. He is, in fact, the God who created everything and needs no such service. Rather, this God challenges all idolatry and will judge those who persist in it once they know the truth. So politely, but emphatically, Paul totally reversed the nature of the occasion. The Athenians presumed to sit in judgement on what they thought was another god who might appreciate their civic favours. But the reality was that they were being confronted with the God who sat in judgement *The God who sits in judgement* upon them and called them, not to a verdict, but to repentance.

This was a bold claim, which may well have sounded arrogant to the council, but Paul supports it first from well chosen quotes from Greek poets, and then by reference to the historical Jesus and his resurrection. At that point the council was divided, as Luke records, between those who contemptuously dismissed the case, and those who wanted to hear more.

The crucial sentence, after Paul's brilliant bridge-building introduction, is: 'Now what you worship as something unknown I am going to proclaim to you' (17:23). When we interpret this in the light of Paul's own development of his theme, we see that Paul *is not* congratulating the Athenians and saying, 'You are really worshipping the true God, though you don't know it'; but rather he is telling them, 'Despite the religiosity of your many gods, you don't *know* the true God at all, though you could and should do, for the knowledge of this God is available before your eyes. But in spite of all your religion, he remains "the unknown god" to you.'[23] Taken thus, it fits perfectly with what Paul writes elsewhere concerning the fact that knowledge of God as Creator is available to human beings, but we have actually suppressed it and chosen ignorance and darkness because of our sin (Rom 1:18-25). God is *not*, in fact, an 'unknown God'; it is the Athenians who are ignorant of him.

There are, however, those who take Paul's meaning in the former sense, i.e. that Paul affirms that underneath all their other gods, the Athenians are in reality worshipping the true God, even if they don't know it. Paul, it is claimed, adopts a very positive and accepting attitude here towards Greek culture and religion by quoting their own poets. On this view, the preaching of Jesus and his resurrection simply brought a fuller understanding of that which the Greeks already worshipped in their own religious cults. Therefore, comes the conclusion, our mission is not to convert idolaters, but to help them see that their religion is in reality the worship of the true God and then fit Christ into that.

Now it is certainly true that Paul quotes from representatives of both Stoic pantheism and from Epicurean deism.[24] But he does so in order to support an affirmation about God that is actually quite different from those authors' original intent. In fact he refers to these philosophies in such a way as to negate their overall claims when set alongside a scriptural (i.e. Old Testament), theistic, creational, world-view. So this is not a generously approving acceptance, but a radical, though still polite, correction of these Greek philosophical and religious views. And it brings Paul to the point of issuing an explicit command to *repent* in view of the imminent judgement of God.

A radical correction

Repentance means turning around, turning away from. Paul is not expecting that the Athenians will express their gratitude that now they know who they are really worshipping, while they return to their 'very religious' idolatry. Rather he wants them to turn away from those idols to the living God, the God who, far from begging for the privilege of the Athenians' patronage, calls them to acknowledge his universal rule and his imminent judgement.

Although the audiences were very different, Paul's position before the educated authorities of Athens was exactly the same as his response to the attempted worship of the less sophisticated crowd at Lystra ('We are ...telling you to turn from these worthless things to the living God...' Note again the emphasis on the availability of the knowledge of God: 14:13-18). And in his testimony in 26:17f, he states that his mission to the Gentiles was 'to open their eyes and turn them from darkness to light and from the power of Satan to God, so that they may receive forgiveness of sins...' This is not the language of one who thought that they were worshipping the true God all along and merely needed to be told so.

Conclusion

The Bible, then, presents us with a far from positive picture of what we call human religions. Religion, like all things human, has good and bad dimensions, but is never portrayed in the Bible as the means of salvation. The Bible is concerned about people and God, and about the need for the nations to recognise who the true and saving God really is – revealed as Yahweh in the Old Testament and in Jesus Christ in the New Testament. It shows us that God can and does speak to people within the framework of religious understanding that they already have. But this is not in order to endorse that prior religion, but to lead beyond it to the fullness of revelation and salvation in Christ.

Conclusion:

At the Checkout

At the Checkout

We began in the supermarket of competing religious ideas. We observed that many people's attitudes to religion now is not very different from their attitude to the products on the shelves of a supermarket. Take your pick and head for the checkout. We have surveyed some of the responses to this supermarket mentality – from those who regard it as basically flawed and dangerous, to those who champion it as the only way to handle the variety. Perhaps it was obvious at the time, but I hope you did notice that the one position I am unable to accept in any form is the relativistic pluralism we looked at in Chapter 4. I do also have serious difficulties with the kind of inclusivism discussed in Chapter 3, but at least I can respect the efforts of its supporters to affirm the centrality and uniqueness of Jesus Christ. It is time, however, to make our own way to the checkout and sort out our purchases. So, in drawing to a conclusion, I would suggest that we need to do at least three things in relation to the truth as we understand it as Christians. We need to clarify our *thinking* about the truth (which is what this book, as part of the Thinking Clearly series, has tried to do). We need to strengthen our *contending* for the truth. And we need to renew our *living* of the truth.

143

Clarify our thinking about the truth

The roots of pluralism   Our opening chapter surveyed some of the cultural plurality of our society, and some of the confused and confusing situations in which this issue of other faiths comes to the surface. We need to recognise the historical roots of this ideological pluralism of western society. We need to understand where the supermarket mentality has come from, if we are going to challenge it effectively. This is not the place to start a new subject, but if you want to think clearly about Christian truth, then you have to think clearly about the things it differs from, including the rise of secularism, humanism, existentialism, and the current flight to postmodernity.[1]

We also need to think biblically about what we mean by 'religion' itself. That was the point of Chapter 6, which was *Clarity about religion*   intended to prevent us from making simplistic, blanket assertions about all religions – either that they are all good, or all the same (the most common popular myth), or that they are all bad and satanic (except Christianity). As we saw, the Bible is not greatly concerned about religious systems as such, but about human beings before God. Religions share in the ambiguity of human response to God – we simultaneously seek after God (being made in God's image), and flee from his presence (being rebellious and disobedient). Religions express and embody both responses, and do not provide us with the means of salvation, for only God has done that.

We also need to think clearly about 'salvation'. On the one hand we must be clear what the human problem is from which *Clarity about salvation*   salvation is needed. If we don't define the problem, we won't have an adequate answer, with the result that salvation can be whatever you want, and any religion can give you it. In Chapter 5 we saw how important the Old Testament background is on this matter. And on the other hand we must challenge the common question, 'Is there salvation in other religions?' and point out that, from a biblical point of view, it is the wrong question. It makes an assumption that is in itself fundamentally unbiblical – namely that salvation is something you get from a religion, and the only problem is, which religion? But according to the Bible, religion does not save anybody. Only God does. And the Bible is the story of what God has done in human history to bring about the salvation of humanity and the whole creation. Salvation is what God has done, not what any religion offers merely as a religion.

Strengthen our contending for the truth

It is significant that the first casualty of the entry of sin into human life was the truth (Gen 3:1-5). And human life ever since has been inclined to 'exchange the truth of God for a lie', expressed, among other things, in the worship of 'created things rather than the Creator' (Rom 1:25). So it is not some kind of lurid exaggeration to detect the marks of satanic deception and lies in human religions, but a sober and biblical recognition that human minds are darkened and perverse. Again, Paul recognises both the spiritual and satanic nature of the causes of our human condition, and, at the same time, the challenge this presents to the preaching of the gospel as a presentation of the truth with the enlightening power of God behind it (2 Cor 4:2-6). *Spiritual warfare* Contending for the truth is a dimension of spiritual warfare and we need to be prepared for that reality.

There are some, however, who dislike such conflict, and particularly revile those who attempt to speak or write in defence of the truth as we understand it from the Bible. I have read mockery in the press of so-called 'self-appointed defenders of the faith', with the added cliche that 'the truth needs no defending'. Of course no Christian is 'self-appointed'. But if we are disciples of Jesus, then we are Christ-appointed *witnesses* to the truth. Of course, in the ultimate sense, God and Christ need no defending by us. Yet in the Bible both Yahweh in the Old Testament and Christ in the New entrusted the truth about themselves and their claims to human witnesses – Israel and the disciples. Witnesses are those who are called upon precisely to speak the truth in a context in which it may be denied or threatened. It is not a matter of arrogance or self-importance, but simply a duty. The prophets, Jesus himself, and the apostles, all warned against the dangers of falsehood and engaged in conflict, dialogue, argument, debate and persuasion. We should not be ashamed to follow their examples. This does not mean, of course, a call to conflict in the worldly sense of viciousness, bitter and extravagant language, personal attack and deceptive manipulation. These are precisely the methods Paul says he had utterly renounced (2 Cor 4:2) and which he warns Timothy against (2 Tim 2:23-26). Our contention for the truth of Christ and the gospel must be with the spiritual weapons which are available for all spiritual warfare, but wielded with love, compassion, gentleness and dignity.

Having made the last point, we need not sit back defensively all the time. Sometimes the best form of defence is attack, and it is perfectly proper to challenge some of the glaring weaknesses in the whole supermarket mentality – i.e. the apparent plausibility of secular western pluralism and its theological mutations.

The fallacies of pluralism We can challenge the relativistic illogic of pluralism. The argument that 'there is no absolute truth' is logically self-contradictory and self-destructive, because it is itself being presented *as* an absolute truth. You cannot be absolutely relative!

We can challenge the hidden arrogance of pluralism. Pluralists say 'Nobody can really know the truth. No religion perceives or contains the truth about the divine reality as it really is.' But how do they *know* that themselves? They are claiming to know a lot about what they say nobody can know. They adopt a stance, as it were, above or behind all other religions and presume to know what those religions may or may not have truthful knowledge about. To put it in more technical terms, what privileged epistemological stance gives the pluralist the right to deny truth and knowledge to any other position than his own? There is, in other words, a hidden arrogance behind the apparent humility of pluralist pronouncements, which shows itself in very explicit intolerance of those who disagree.

We can challenge the cultural short-sightedness of pluralism. Modern western pluralism, as an ideology, is a particular cultural development of the post-Enlightenment era in Europe and North America. Yet it claims to have the key to all human knowledge and religion. But by what right? We need to remember, as we saw in Chapter 4, that what pluralism does to Christianity it does to all other religions as well, and all in the name of a peculiarly reductionist view of truth which is not shared by the vast majority of the human race. So Christians, along with other great religious traditions which make exclusive truth claims (in the sense defined in Chapter 2), have every right to challenge such thinking and expose its cultural arrogance.

The conflict over truth can be costly. Since spiritual warfare is involved, we know we are not engaged merely in a polite discussion about ideas, but are *Prepared to suffer* challenging the realm of falsehood where the Evil One defends his territory. To do so can be painful, violent and costly. Throughout history, and still today, those who call Jesus Lord and refuse to share his lordship with any other claimants, have suffered for such a stand.

In western countries we rightly cherish our democratic freedoms and the climate of social and political toleration which allows and even encourages the religious plurality that we surveyed in Chapter 1. Perhaps we easily forget how comparatively recent and unusual such a state of affairs actually is. Religious freedom of the western sort is a relatively recent phenomenon, a kind of love-child of that curious union of gospel truth and Enlightenment liberties. But it may turn out to be a blip in history, not a permanently secure social reality. Pluralism itself is becoming a new dogma, and in some contexts it can be experienced as just as intolerant and repressive as the alleged religious bigotries it claims to replace. Those who insist on declaring, however humbly and non-aggressively, their allegiance to Jesus Christ as *only* Lord, God, and Saviour, find themselves facing opposition, exclusion and legal threat. This happens in the educational world and may spread to other areas of public life. 'Political correctness' can be horrendously dogmatic and intolerant. There is legitimate concern over the appropriateness of various methods of evangelism, but the day may not be far off when any form of evangelism at all among communities of other faiths will be made illegal on the grounds of social and racial harmony. Are we prepared for such developments? And are we willing to learn from the experience of sisters and brothers in those parts of the world where such danger, persecution, and legal constriction are a normal part of everyday life for Christians?

Renew our living of the truth

The courage of the first Christians

The earliest followers of Jesus faced the twin worlds of Jerusalem and Rome, of Jewish hostility and Gentile power. They faced these ancient and vast religious and imperial realities with the claim that Jesus of Nazareth, a crucified Galilean carpenter, was God incarnate, the only true Saviour of humanity, and the risen Lord of the whole universe. And they stood firm in that conviction and message until the world came to know it, believe it, and be transformed by it. And we must not underestimate the astounding nature of that achievement. The first century world of the Mediterranean civilisation was as much a kaleidoscope of religious and cultural plurality as anything we know in the West today. It was awash with gods, myths, philosophies, cults, mystic rites and orders, hopes and fears. And in the midst of that the Christians proclaimed a historical person as the final truth and only Saviour, and had the courage to live and die for that faith. Our generation faces a similar challenge and will need to pray for comparable courage.

Confidence in the truth

It is so important that we do not cave in to the popular idea that all religions are a matter of human opinion and belief, subjective fancies that may be nice for you and your friends, but need not be true for me and mine. Paul was so urgent in saying that his message was precisely not that kind of thing. The Greek world was full of 'sophists' – men who travelled around peddling their bright ideas and getting paid for lectures on the latest theories. No, said Paul; 'We preach Christ crucified.' The gospel announces facts, witnessed events in recorded history. The gospel is good news, not good ideas, or even good ideals. There is an objectivity, a 'having-happened-ness', about it, which must not be reduced to a mere 'feel-good factor'. Unfortunately even Christians turn their evangelism into something less than the New Testament model and concentrate only on 'What Jesus means to me,' or 'This is how

Jesus met my needs; try him and see if he will meet yours.'

But the New Testament declaration of the gospel is to say 'God so loved the world that he gave his only Son.' It is to affirm, 'God was in Christ reconciling the world to himself.' It is to maintain that 'Christ died for our sins according to the Scriptures, that he was buried and that he was raised on the third day, according to the Scriptures.' It is to marvel that 'While we were yet sinners, Christ died for us.' And, conversely, it is to be convinced that 'If Christ is *not* raised, then our message is empty and your faith is empty.'

There is no arrogance in all of this, for the gospel is not something we invented, or can take credit for. It is not a matter of boasting, 'We've got a better religion than yours,' but of simple affirmation, 'There *is* a gospel – and it confronts all of us with the massive reality of the God who is the Creator of all, the judge of all, the lover of all, and who died for all.'

We need to regain our confidence in the reality and truth of the gospel we say we believe. It is not true because we believe it. We believe it because we have met the Truth. 'Capital T Truth' is not dead, as the postmodernist wants us to accept. Capital T Truth *died … and rose again*.

It has been said that the church should be the 'plausibility structure' for the truth of the gospel. That is to say, the church should be such a community of life and practice that it makes the gospel *believable*. There is little point proclaiming how the gospel is *true* if people cannot see that it *works*. The fact of our contemporary western world is that for many people Christianity is not so much regarded as untrue (in the sense that they have considered its claims and rejected them for rational reasons), as simply implausible. It doesn't fit with the dominant cultural norms and assumptions of our society, and there is no plausible alternative community that demonstrates the truth of the gospel by actually living it out in such powerfully persuasive ways that people recognise the truth of the message in the distinctiveness of the life. That was a substantial part of the reason for the evangelistic success of the church in Acts, as Luke points out.

Ultimately, the most powerful way to communicate the truth of

Moral and spiritual renewal

the uniqueness of Jesus is not so much to argue for it (which this book may at least help!), as to live like him. And the great thing is that this is open to every Christian man and woman, boy and girl. It is not the prerogative of specialists, theologians, academics, clergy. In fact it is far too important to be left to them. As we said above, God entrusts the truth of his revelation and his salvation to *witnesses*. 'And you shall be my witnesses,' said Jesus, to all his disciples. That is our privilege and responsibility. Thinking clearly matters a lot. Living it out matters more.

Mahatma Gandhi is reputed to have said that if all the Christians were to live like Jesus, India would no longer be Hindu. The tragedy was that they did not, and so the uniqueness of Christ is not the powerfully attractive reality that it could and should be.

It was said about the early Christians of the first few centuries that the reason why they eventually won over the Roman empire was that they 'out-thought, out-lived and out-died' their opponents. That is, they had better answers to the great problems of humanity than the religions and philosophies which surrounded them. But they also lived better lives and demonstrated the moral power and dynamic of the Christian faith. And they were prepared to pay the ultimate cost rather than surrender the truth of the gospel and the uniqueness of Jesus. Thinking clearly about the uniqueness of Jesus calls for no smaller commitment in our own day.

References

References

Chapter 1

1. The use of 'plurality' here is deliberately intended to distinguish between the obvious fact of many religious communities living together, and the ideology or philosophy of 'pluralism' as a theory about the truth or validity of the world's religions. Unfortunately, the term 'religious pluralism' is frequently used in both senses. That is, sometimes it is used to describe the social mixture of religions, and sometimes it is used to advocate the view that all religions are in some way true and valid. This is confusing since it is perfectly possible to accept *plurality* in the first sense (there is not much else one can do!) while rejecting *pluralism* in the second sense. On the whole, I shall try to maintain this distinction of terminology in what follows. Similar distinctions can be observed, e.g. between duality and dualism, community and communism, etc.

2. A. Race, *Christians and Religious Pluralism* (Maryknoll: Orbis, 1982) p. 29.

3. A. Race, *Christians and Religious Pluralism,* p. 137. Race is very concerned not to be embarrassed by his Christianity. So he prefers to interpret the New Testament language mythically in order to avoid the idea of God actually having intervened in the

153

history of this world. He dislikes talk of God sending his Son or becoming human: 'The metaphors of "sending" or "becoming" imply that God acts from outside to intervene in a world which, viewed scientifically and historically, is seen normally as a closed web of cause and effect. [The incarnation story] ... presupposes an interventionist framework of divine action which is now regarded by the majority of theologians as redundant (p. 118).

Apart from disputing his 'majority of theologians' claim, I would comment that Race is caught up in a myth of his own. That is, he is interpreting one set of affirmations (the New Testament) as myth, in order to avoid conflict with what he takes to be fact but is actually one of the great myths of our modern, post-Enlightenment age, namely the allegedly scientific assumption of a 'closed', mechanistic universe. Even for many scientists this is now recognised as an inadequate and reductionist model for understanding the natural universe itself, let alone the complexity of human history on this planet. Compare, for example, the writings of John Polkinghorne, including his recent survey of three 'scientist theologians', *Scientists as Theologians* (London: SPCK, 1996).

4. See J. Hick (ed), *The Myth of God Incarnate* (London: SCM, 1977); and the prompt response edited by Michael Green, *The Truth of God Incarnate* (London: Hodder and Stoughton, 1977). See also the substantial books listed in Chapter 5, note 9.

5. Thus, for example, the pluralist theologian Paul Knitter, when he comes to explain how his vision of 'unitive pluralism' can fit with a unique Jesus, has to adopt a wholly 'mythic' interpretation of New Testament language, along with an 'experiential' interpretation of the resurrection, in order to end up with what he calls a 'non-normative Christology', *No Other Name: A Critical Survey of Christian Attitudes Towards the World Religions* (London: SCM, 1985), chapter 9. Similarly, it is not accidental that the celebrated book edited by John Hick, *The Myth of God Incarnate* (London: SCM, 1977) concludes with the chapter 'Jesus and the World Religions' in which Hick puts forward his pluralist position.

Chapter 2

1. The three terms, exclusivism, inclusivism and pluralism, were used by Alan Race, *Christians and Religious Pluralism* (Maryknoll: Orbis, 1982). They were used again by the Anglican Inter-Faith Consultative Group of the Board of Mission and Unity of the General Synod when they produced their report, *Towards a Theology for Inter-Faith Dialogue* (London: 1984, hereafter called the BMU report). Another very helpful discussion of the three terms, which, like the BMU report favours inclusivism, is, Gavin D'Costa, *Theology and Religious Pluralism* (Oxford: Blackwell, 1986). A much more detailed classification of different Christian responses to the question is given by Paul Knitter, *No Other Name? A Critical Survey of Christian Attitudes towards the World Religions* (Maryknoll: Orbis, and London: SCM, 1985). Knitter himself argues for pluralism. An evangelical critique of inclusivism and pluralism which sets out a strong case for exclusivism is Harold Netland, *Dissonant Voices: Religious Pluralism and the Question of Truth* (Grand Rapids: Eerdmans, and Leicester: Apollos, 1991).

2. H. Netland, *Dissonant Voices,* pp. 9-10.

3. John Polkinghorne, a renowned scientist as well as theologian, gives another example: 'We certainly do not want to be triumphalistic, but nor do we wish to forget that there may well be issues on which we are right and those who do not share our view are mistaken. In the end, it is the question of truth that matters, and there is an inevitable exclusivity about truth. If you tell me that you hold the view that the phenomenon of heat is due to the subtle fluid caloric, I do not say that you are entitled to your opinion and I respect you for it. I try, instead, to convince you of the correctness of the kinetic theory of heat energy. Either Jesus is God's Lord and Christ or he is not, and it matters supremely to know which is the right judgement.' *Science and Christian Belief: Theological Reflections of a Bottom-up Thinker* (London: SPCK, 1994), p. 191.

4. It is important to recognise this because sometimes exclusivists are accused of being in bondage to a western understanding of the nature of truth, i.e. that we insist on exclusive alternatives (a statement is *either* true *or* it is not) whereas other cultures are more open to see both possibilities. However, while we certainly need to recognise that truth is a much bigger reality than merely factual propositions, it is nevertheless a universal fact that any truth claim is exclusive by nature. Sometimes this is called 'the law of non-contradiction', which states that any proposition (*p*) and its contradiction (*not p*) cannot both be true at the same time and in the same context. This is not just a peculiar western idea; human thought and communication universally operate on this principle, or else they become totally nonsensical. This is because it is impossible to deny the law of non-contradiction without assuming its truth. The person who wants to say that in the religious dimension of life, for example, 'it *is* possible for *p* and *not p* to be simultaneously true' has made a proposition. If his proposition is true, then he must accept that its opposite is also true, and thus he has to accept the denial of his own affirmation, which means accepting the law of non-contradiction. If this sounds complicated, a better explanation is found in Netland, *Dissonant Voices,* ch. 4, and especially pp. 141-150. See also a strong defence of the universal validity of the non-contradiction principle by A. Kirk, *Loosing the Chains: Religion as Opium and Liberation* (London: Hodder and Stoughton, 1992), pp. 58-62.

5. The BMU report summarised exclusivism in this way: 'The Christian exclusivist theory counts all religions other than Christianity as the product of blindness or even sinful unbelief. At the very extreme this is expressed by saying that they are the work of Satan. At best, other religions represent the fruit of God's activity in nature and conscience, which is distorted by sin and human pride. Consequently, they are either wholly in error or simply inadequate for salvation and reflect nothing of the real saving grace of God. On this understanding, the doctrine of the incarnation of Christ places Christianity in opposition to or discontinuity with the other religions. Christ alone is the Saviour

who has revealed perfectly the heart and mind of the Father and the true way of discipleship. Those who do not acknowledge this word of truth therefore stand under judgement. Moreover this judgement applies equally to the church when it is seen to be acting without reliance on God's grace given in the incarnation. For exclusivism, then, the absolute supremacy of Christ is a given part of the data of Christian identity' (para. 16).

6. Barth's views on this matter are conveniently expressed in his lecture, 'The Revelation of God as the Abolition of Religion', in J. Hick and B. Hebblethwaite (eds.), *Christianity and Other Religions* (Fortress, 1980), pp. 32-51. This way of viewing the relationship of Christianity to other faiths was the dominant one in the World Council of Churches, from its missionary orientated beginning in Edinburgh in 1910, through Jerusalem in 1928, and especially at Tambaram (Madras) in 1938. At that time it was heavily influenced by the writing of the Dutch missiologist Hendrik Kraemer, who, in line with the theology of Karl Barth, stressed the theme of the *discontinuity* between God's revelation in Christ and all other religions. See H. Kraemer, *The Christian Message in a Non-Christian World* (Edinburgh House Press, 1938), especially ch. IV 'The Attitude towards the Non-Christian Religions', pp. 101-141.

In fact, this remained much to the fore in WCC theology up to the retirement of Visser't Hooft as General Secretary in 1966 (e.g. his book, *No Other Name*, [London: SCM, 1963]).

In a more modified form, exclusivism is also the major thrust of the writings of two influential British missiologists, Lesslie Newbigin (e.g. *The Open Secret,* [Eerdmans, 1978]; 2nd revised edition, 1995) and Stephen Neill (e.g. *The Christian Faith and Other Faiths,* [Oxford, 1961], and *The Supremacy of Jesus*, [Hodder and Stoughton, 1984]). Newbigin and Neill would not identify with some forms of the exclusivist position, however, and for that reason Knitter, in his survey, locates them not in his 'Conservative Evangelical Model', but among what he calls 'Mainline Protestants'.

7. Race, *Christians and Religious Pluralism,* p. 24.

8. Among the many who hold this position, the most recent and accessible include, John Piper, *Let the Nations Be Glad: The Supremacy of God in Missions* (Leicester: Apollos, 1993), and Don Carson, *The Gagging of God: Christianity Confronts Pluralism* (Leicester: Apollos, 1996).

9. See John Sanders, *No Other Name: An Investigation into the Destiny of the Unevangelized* (Grand Rapids: Eerdmans, 1992), ch 2, pp. 37-59. This gives a full account of the position, with a presentation and critique of its biblical and theological arguments, and a historical bibliography of those who have advocated it in the past and present.

10. For a strong critique of this particular distortion, see also Don Carson, *The Gagging of God: Christianity Confronts Pluralism*, pp. 289-291.

11. John Piper argues against this use of the Old Testament saints to show that people can be saved without knowing about the historical Jesus Christ. He stresses the 'tremendously important turn in redemptive history' that took place with the incarnation of Jesus and with his cross and resurrection. 'The coming of Jesus Christ into the world is an event of such stupendous proportions that a change has occurred in the necessary focus of saving faith.' So even if in the ages before Christ God 'overlooked' the ignorance of the nations, now, in the age since the incarnation, only faith in Christ can be salvific (*Let the Nations be Glad: The Supremacy of God in Missions,* pp. 127-135). However, although it is of course vitally important to see the centrality of Christ in the salvation history of the Bible and to recognise that he did indeed inaugurate the new age of God's saving purpose for humanity, I cannot see that this puts *those who never do or can know about Jesus* in any different position before God from those who lived historically BC and outside the sphere of special revelation in Israel. It cannot be the case that God operates differently in response to those who never in their lifetime know about Jesus, but live chronologically after his coming, from those who never knew about him because they lived chronologically before his

coming. They are equally living, from their own point of view, in 'times of ignorance' as far as the gospel is concerned. Therefore, it seems to me, whatever understanding we arrive at regarding the possibility or otherwise of people being saved BC it is in principle extensible to those who, though living AD, are in reality 'informationally BC'. And conversely, if we deny even the possibility of any person today being saved who has not heard of Jesus, on what grounds can we affirm the salvation of Enoch, Noah, Melchizedek, etc. (i.e., those who were not beneficiaries of the special redemptive revelation of God to Israel)? I am not convinced that even Don Carson's thorough discussion of the matter adequately answers this question (*The Gagging of God: Christianity Confronts Pluralism,* pp. 297-299).

12. This is the view advocated by Norman Anderson, e.g. in *Christianity and World Religions* (Leicester: IVP, 1970; 2nd revised edition, 1984); John Stott, in D. L. Edwards and J. R. W. Stott, *Essentials: A liberal-evangelical dialogue* (London: Hodder and Stoughton, 1988), pp. 320-329; Peter Cotterell, *Mission and Meaninglessness: The Good News in a World of Suffering and Disorder* (London: SPCK, 1990), pp. 75-83.

13. I certainly prefer to regard this position (ii) as a variety of exclusivism (since it undoubtedly maintains that salvation is exclusively available in and through the work of Christ). Others, however, and especially Sanders (*No Other Name,* ch. 7), have recently labelled this position as well as the next (iii), 'inclusivism'. Carson calls the 'Possibly yes' view, 'soft inclusivism', and the next position ('Definitely yes' – advocated by Sanders and Pinnock), 'hard inclusivism' (*The Gagging of God,* pp. 278-314), though he does say that 'soft inclusivism' is 'barely distinguishable from exclusivism' (p. 279) – with which I agree.

Perhaps it would be better, if the term inclusivism is going to be used for either of positions (ii) and (iii) that it is qualified as 'evangelical inclusivism', since it is certainly put forward by those who claim fundamental allegiance to the central evangelical affirmation of salvation through Christ alone and by grace alone (and are therefore, in that sense, exclusivist). I prefer, however, to retain the term inclusivism for the view that sees some lesser or greater salvific value in *other religions as such*, even while asserting that ultimately all such salvation is somehow centred on, or normatively defined by, Christ. This view (as exemplified by Karl Rahner's 'anonymous Christianity') seems significantly different and it is a position with which I have much greater difficulty, as the discussion in the next chapter indicates.

14. C. H. Pinnock, *A Wideness in God's Mercy: The Finality of Jesus Christ in a World of Religions* (Grand Rapids: Zondervan, 1992), and J. Oswald Sanders, *No Other Name: An Investigation into the Destiny of the Unevangelized* (Grand Rapids: Eerdmans, 1992). Cf. also, J. Oswald Sanders (ed.), *What About Those Who Have Never Heard? Three Views on the Destiny of the Unevangelized* (Downers Grove: IVP, 1995).

15. See the presentations of this point of view as an interpretation of a range of biblical texts in C. Pinnock, *A Wideness in God's Mercy,* pp. 17-35; and J. O. Sanders, *No Other Name,* pp. 217-224. Cf. also Sanders' briefer exposition in 'Evangelical Responses to Salvation Outside the Church', *Christian Scholars Review* 24:1 (1994), pp. 45-58.

16. Some people solve this problem by proposing that there will be an opportunity for all who did not hear of Christ in their lifetime to be confronted with him after death. At that point, their response to Christ will confirm the response they would have made if they had heard in life, and they will be saved or condemned on that basis. There are variations on this idea of a 'post-mortem encounter', but the strongest recent presentation of it is in C. Pinnock, *A Wideness in God's Mercy,* pp. 169-172. For other alternatives, see J. O. Sanders, *No Other Name,* chs. 5-6. In my view this theory rests on very fragile biblical evidence, and strikes me as either demeaning of God's knowledge (if it implies that God needs to wait to see what response people might make to Christ), or unnecessary in any case (if God already knows what

response people *would have made* if they *had* heard of Christ, what further purpose does a post-mortem encounter serve?).

17. Carson rightly points out that greater caution is required in interpreting the texts which speak of God's desire for the salvation of 'all'. In some cases it is clear that it is the impartiality of God's saving love that is meant – as in the case of Peter's response to Cornelius: God accepts Gentiles as well as Jews, and so in that sense accepts any and all (see Chapter 6 for a discussion of Acts 10: 34-35). In others it is probably right to infer that the text means 'all without distinction' rather than 'all without exception'. See *The Gagging of God,* pp. 287-289.

18. Sanders' explanation of God's dealings with Pharaoh, for example, as salvific in intention if not in result ('God was trying to evangelise the Egyptians'), seems quite bizarre to me. See Sanders' chapter in G. Fackre, R. H. Nash and J. O. Sanders, *What About Those Who Have Never Heard* (Downers Grove: IVP, 1995), pp. 26-27.

19. On this point, see Carson, *The Gagging of God*, pp. 296-297.

20. One might argue that the saved from the pre-Columbus Americas (for example) would not quite be 'none at all', if one were to take the position that the total number of the elect will include not only those who have both been evangelised and have responded, but also 'elect infants dying in infancy' (to use the phrase of the Westminster Confession of Faith). One could, presumably, populate this elect and saved category with infants from all nations who have been saved by virtue of dying before moral consciousness and therefore before the necessity of repentance. But it is hard to avoid the feeling that this quite conjectural concession which lacks any clear biblical evidence somewhat dilutes the thrust of the scriptural portrayal of the God who longs for all to come to repentance and salvation.

21. Carson would therefore probably list me under this category of 'soft inclusivists'. I would resist the latter term, however,

since, as I have explained, it seems better to reserve 'inclusivism' for those who affirm or allow for the possibility of a Christ-centred salvation in and through other faiths, and that is a view I find difficult to define or defend (see the next chapter) and certainly do not share. Perhaps I would be happier with 'soft, or non-restrictivist, exclusivist!'

Chapter 3

1. This is frequently linked to a theology of the universal enlightening of all human beings by the *logos* ('The Word' in John 1). This is discussed in Chapter 6.

2. For a critique of the inclusivist arguments of the BMU report, particularly in relation to its use of the Bible, see Chris Wright, 'Inter Faith Dialogue', *Anvil* 1.3 (1984), pp. 231-258.

3. Knitter in his survey of different models, describes this as 'The Mainline Protestant Model'; see *No Other Name?*, ch. VI, pp. 97-119. He includes within this category a study of such theologians as Paul Althaus, Emil Brunner, Pannenberg and Carl Braaten, as well as the missiologists Stephen Neill and Lesslie Newbigin.

4. Originally, of course, this declaration was directed primarily at heretics and schismatics within the wider world of broadly Christian traditions, not at other world religions as we now know them.

5. The four most important documents of Vatican II as regards the question of Christianity and other faiths were: *Lumen Gentium*, 'Dogmatic Constitution on the Church'; *Nostra Aetate*, 'Declaration on the Relationship of the Church to Non-Christian Religions'; *Gaudium et Spes*, 'Pastoral Constitution'; *Ad gentes*, 'Decree on the Church's Missionary Activity'. The full texts can be consulted in A. Flannery (ed.), *Vatican II: The Conciliar and Post-Conciliar Documents* (Collegeville: MN, 1984, and Leominster: Fowler-Wright, 1985).

6. For discussion of the Roman Catholic inclusivist view on other religions, see P. Cotterell, *Mission and Meaninglessness: The Good News in a World of Suffering and Disorder* (London: SPCK, 1990), pp. 40-52; and D. Wright, 'The Watershed of Vatican II: Catholic Approaches to Religious Pluralism', in A. D. Clarke and B. W. Winter, *One God, One Lord: Christianity in a World of Religious Pluralism* (2nd ed. Grand Rapids: Baker, and Carlisle: Paternoster, 1992), pp. 207-226.

7. *Lumen Gentium* 16.

8. *Nostra Aetate* 2.

9. Rahner's work spanned many years and produced many volumes of *Theological Investigations* (London: Darton, Longman and Todd). However, he summarised his central views on this matter in a lecture published as 'Christianity and the Non-Christian Religions', in J. Hick and B. Hebblethwaite (eds.), *Christianity and Other Religions* (Glasgow: Collins Fontana, 1980), pp. 52-79. A helpful summary and discussion of Rahner's position can be found in M. Barnes, *Religions in Conversation* (London: SPCK, 1989).

10. K. Rahner, *Theological Investigations* Vol. V, pp. 121, 125.

11. P. Cotterell, *Mission and Meaninglessness,* p. 50.

12. P. Cotterell, *Mission and Meaninglessness*, p. 51. The danger of being romantically optimistic about religion in general is noted also by C. Pinnock (even though his own position is not very different in result, if not in its theological premises, from Rahner's); cf. *A Wideness in God's Mercy,* pp. 84-92. See also the sharp critique of religion by A. Kirk, *Loosing the Chains: Religion as Opium and Liberation* (Sevenoaks: Hodder and Stoughton, 1992).

13. J. E. Goldingay and C. J. H. Wright, 'Yahweh our God, Yahweh One', in A. D. Clarke and B. W. Winter (eds.), *One God, One Lord,* p. 54.

14. Race: *Pluralism*, p. 54.

15. It is important to note the last comment. Some strong rebuttals of the pluralist agenda have come, not only from exclusivist and evangelical sources, but also from inclusivists. Gavin D'Costa, for example, another Roman Catholic inclusivist theologian, edited the volume *Christian Uniqueness Reconsidered*, with its provocative sub-title, *The Myth of a Pluralistic Theology of Religions* (Maryknoll: Orbis, 1990). The book is a scholarly riposte to the pluralist symposium, J. Hick and P. F. Knitter, *The Myth of Christian Uniqueness* (Maryknoll: Orbis, 1987 and London: SCM, 1988). D'Costa's own contribution to the book 'Christ, the Trinity and Religious Plurality' (pp. 16-29), develops an interesting and instructive trinitarian approach to the question. However, it relies heavily on the assumption of the role of the Spirit of God in and among the world religions that seems to go beyond, or have no clearly defined relation to, the biblical emphasis on the link between the work of the Spirit and the person of Christ. There seems to be a dissipation of the distinctness of the historical salvation and revelation of God in Christ. As the Indian scholar, K. Gnanakan, comments: 'The problem with the inclusivist position is that there is very little difference between what one is asked to accept as the work of God and Jesus Christ in other religions, and the inherent value of that religion in itself. If God's work is available even outside Jesus Christ, why then was Jesus' work necessary? There needs to be some restrictions even for the 'normativeness' of Christ to be considered, or else everything can be justified as God's revelation.' *The Pluralist Predicament* (Bangalore: Theological Book Trust, 1992), p. 85.

16. See, however, the discussion in Chapter 2, notes 12 and 20, over the confusion regarding 'inclusivism' when used of evangelicals. This chapter has not been concerned with what some scholars (Sanders, Carson, etc.) refer to as 'inclusivism', but which I prefer to call 'non-restrictivist exclusivism'.

Chapter 4

1. A. Race, *Pluralism,* p. 78.

2. J. Hick, *God has Many Names* (London: Macmillan, 1980), p. 52. Theocentric pluralism is also espoused in various nuanced forms by the Indian theologians R. Panikkar and S. Samartha, by Wilfred Cantwell Smith, and by the two authors already quoted several times so far – Alan Race and Paul Knitter. A thorough exposition and critique of the work of the two Indian scholars above, Panikkar and Samartha, along with the Sri Lankan, Aloysius Pieris, is provided by V. Ramachandra, *The Recovery of Mission: Beyond the Pluralist Paradigm* (Carlisle: Paternoster, 1996).

3. I am confining myself here to some fundamental theological issues raised by pluralism. There are many other aspects in which it is open to profound criticism and which are tackled by other scholars. Cf. L. Newbigin, *The Gospel in a Pluralist Society* (London: SPCK, 1989); H. Netland, *Dissonant Voices;* J. A. Kirk, *Loosing the Chains.*

4. Hick uses the term *personae* for this, which originally in Latin referred to the mask which ancient actors wore. Thus, what the worshippers of a particular deity 'see' as they contemplate their particular god is not the divine reality as it really is in itself (the actor), but only the 'mask' as a kind of interface between the hidden divine reality (the actor) and the worshipper (the spectator). This assumes, of course, that although the different religions have manifestly different and grossly contrasting 'masks', it is the same actor behind all of them. Then he goes on to suggest using *impersonae* for the non-personal understandings of the ultimate, as found, for example in philosophical *advaita* Hinduism and Buddhism.

5. J. Hick, 'A Religious Understanding of Religion', in D. Cohn-Sherbok (ed.), *Many Mansions: Interfaith and Religious Intolerance* (London: Bellew, 1992), pp. 122-136, (quotation

from pp. 130-131). A fuller explanation of Hick's thinking in this area will be found in his more recent substantial statement of his religious philosophy, *An Interpretation of Religion: Human Responses to the Transcendent* (London: Macmillan, 1989) especially Part Four, pp. 233-296.

6. See, L. Newbigin, *The Open Secret: An Introduction to the Theology of Mission* (rev. ed., Grand Rapids: Eerdmans, and London: SPCK, 1995), pp. 165-167.

7. Race, *Pluralism,* p. 136.

8. Panikkar has been quite influential and is part of the circle of pluralist scholars who have contributed to the symposium edited by Hick, *The Myth of Christian Uniqueness*. His theology is surveyed by P. Knitter, *No Other Name?,* ch. 8, and given a more critical assessment by V. Ramachandra, *The Recovery of Mission,* ch. 3.

9. R. Panikkar, *The Trinity and the Religious Experience of Man,* (Maryknoll: Orbis, 1973). For a survey of Panikkar's views, see also Knitter, *No Other Name?* ch. 8.

10. A. G. Hunter, *Christianity and Other Faiths in Britain* (London: SCM, 1985), p. 55.

11. *Ibid.* p. 76.

12. Quoted in J. Hick and B. Hebblethwaite (eds.), *Christianity and Other Religions* (Glasgow: Collins, 1980), p. 186.

13. Some pluralists are indeed prepared to say that the worship of Christ is actually idolatry, though they carefully redefine idolatry in a positive light, and tend to be very dismissive of how the Bible talks of it. Wilfred Cantwell Smith, for example, in a carefully argued reassessment of what, on a pluralist under-standing, actually constitutes idolatry, says that it should only be used negatively when describing religious positions which

regard themselves as ultimate and then negate the value of others.

On such grounds, 'For Christians to think that Christianity is true, final, or salvific, is a form of idolatry' if by that they mean to deny that God has also inspired Islam, Hinduism, etc. He goes on to ask whether 'the figure of Christ served as ... an idol through the centuries for Christians?' and essentially answers that it has, but there is nothing wrong with that since the best meaning of idols in all religions is something earthly or material in itself which becomes the channel of transcendence. See W. Cantwell Smith, 'Idolatry in Comparative Perspective', in John Hick and Paul F. Knitter (eds.), *The Myth of Christian Uniqueness,* pp. 53-68; and cf. also the comments of Tom F. Driver, in the same volume, 'I think it necessary to say that the idolisation of Christ – let us call it "Christidolatry" – is not only possible but in fact frequent. Indeed I would go further and say that there is even such a thing as an idolatrous devotion to God' (pp. 214-215). It will be clear from my own comments in Chapter 6 that I prefer still to maintain a biblical understanding of the category of idolatry as meaning the action of giving ultimate and divine status to anything or anyone that is not in reality the living God – meaning the God as revealed in the Bible, not the characterless, abstract 'Transcendent' of the pluralist hypothesis. On this understanding, the worship of anything or anyone other than God as revealed in Christ *is* idolatry, but the worship of Christ himself as not merely the one through whom we can 'see' God, but ontologically God-in-humanity, is assuredly *not*.

14. Muslims are well aware of the implications of the pluralist developments in Christian theology. A friend from Singapore has told me that *The Myth of God Incarnate* is required reading for Muslim missionaries. I was told by Indian Christian missionaries in India that even in remote rural villages Muslims can counter the Christian gospel with the riposte that even bishops in the Church of England now believe what Muslims have always believed – that Jesus was not really God and did not really rise again.

Chapter 5

1. I have tried to present a detailed survey of how Jesus drew his sense of identity, mission and values from his Hebrew Scriptures, in, Chris Wright, *Knowing Jesus through the Old Testament,* (London: Harper Collins, 1992, and Downers Grove: IVP, 1995). The chapters of this book include, Jesus and the Old Testament Story, Jesus and the Old Testament Promise, Jesus and his Old Testament Identity, Jesus and his Old Testament Mission, Jesus and his Old Testament Values. It also includes a bibliography of significant works, Jewish and Christian, on the historical Jesus and his relation to the Hebrew Scriptures and first century Judaism.

2. By starting with a discussion of sin and salvation, I am by no means overlooking the importance of the creation material in the Bible and its relevance to Christian relations with people of other faiths. A lot can be said on the image of God in all human beings, on the fact that all humans are addressable by and accountable to the one living God, and on the relevance of the Wisdom literature, with its creation orientation, to the inter-faith question. Some of this is surveyed in Chapter 6. For a fuller discussion, see John Goldingay and Christopher Wright, 'Yahweh our God, Yahweh One: The Old Testament and Religious Pluralism', in Andrew D. Clarke and Bruce W. Winter (eds.), *One God, One Lord in a World of Religious Pluralism,* pp. 34-52. The focus of our discussion here, however, is the redemptive uniqueness of Christ, not the whole breadth of the Old Testament's contribution to our understanding of other faiths.

3. For a helpful discussion of this, see, J. R. Middleton and B. J. Walsh, *Truth is Stranger Than it Used to Be: Biblical Faith in a Postmodern Age* (London: SPCK, 1995).

4. J. Hick, *An Interpretation of Religion,* p. 301. This is a curiously elitist view of salvation, in that it is modelled by the exceptions, rather than freely available to all.

5. This is one point where the pluralist assumption that all religions can be equally salvifically effective really begs enormous questions. For in the end (literally) death will reveal the truth or falsehood of some or all religious teachings. Thus, if at death we are extinguished totally, then all religions with any teaching that salvation involves an after-life will be proved false. If we return to another reincarnated form of life on the present unredeemed earth, Christianity will be proved wrong. If we stand before the God and Father of our Lord Jesus Christ as described in the Bible, then other religions will be proved wrong. In other words, death must surely demonstrate the exclusive nature of truth! In any bounded set of divergent (i.e. mutually contradictory) statements about the same reality, it is possible that all the statements are false, or that one of them is true and all the others false. What is not possible is that all of them are true. Multiple choice questions in examinations rely on this fundamental principle! For example, I may say, 'My age today is 35, or 43, or 49, or 51, or 56, or 57.' They may all be untrue. But if one is true, the others cannot be. What is impossible is that they are all simultaneously true.

6. Carl Braaten, 'The Uniqueness and Universality of Jesus Christ', in G. H. Anderson and T. F. Stransky (eds.), *Faith Meets Faith,* Mission Trends, No. 5, (New York: Paulist Press, and Grand Rapids: Eerdmans, 1981), pp. 69-89.

7. E.g. Amos 9:7; Deut 2:20-23; Ex 9:13-16; Is 10:5-19; Jer 27:5-7; Is 44:28 – 45:13.

8. This comparison has been thoroughly examined by David Ball, 'The "I am" Sayings of Jesus and Religious Pluralism', in A. D. Clarke and B. W. Winter (eds,), *One God, One Lord,* pp. 65-84.

9. See, for example, the following works of established and reputed scholars in the New Testament field: R. T. France, 'The Worship of Jesus: a Neglected Factor in Christological Debate?' in H. H. Rowdon (ed.), *Christ the Lord: Studies in Christology*

presented to Donald Guthrie (Leicester: IVP, 1982), pp. 17-36; *ibid,* 'Development in New Testament Christology' *Themelios* 18.1 (1992), pp. 4-8; J. B. Green and M. Turner (eds.), *Jesus of Nazareth Lord and Christ: Essays on the Historical Jesus and New Testament Christology* (Grand Rapids: Eerdmans, and Carlisle: Paternoster, 1994); M. Harris, *Jesus as God: The New Testament Use of 'Theos' in Reference to Jesus* (Grand Rapids: Baker, 1992); L. Hurtado, *One God, One Lord: Early Christian Devotion and Ancient Jewish Monotheism* (London: SCM, and Philadelphia: Fortress, 1988); *ibid,* 'The origins of the worship of Christ', *Themelios* 19.2 (1994), pp. 4-8; I. H. Marshall, *I Believe in the Historical Jesus* (London: Hodder and Stoughton, and Grand Rapids: Eerdmans, 1979); *ibid, The Origins of New Testament Christology* (Leicester and Downers Grove: IVP, 1976, 1990); C. F. D. Moule, *The Origin of Christology* (Cambridge: CUP, 1977); B. Witherington III, *The Christology of Jesus* (Minneapolis: Fortress, 1990); N. T. Wright, *Who Was Jesus?* (London: SPCK, 1992).

Chapter 6

1. *Threskeia* in James 1:26f refers to practical behaviour, not to systems of belief or ritual. The nearest to our modern use of the term is Acts 26:5, where Paul uses it of his whole background in Judaism.

2. J. Blauw, 'The Biblical View of Man in his Religion', in G. H. Anderson (ed.), *The Theology of the Christian Mission* (London: SCM, 1961), p. 32, (writing before the advent of compulsory inclusive language!).

3. J. Blauw, *The Missionary Nature of the Church,* (McGraw Hill, 1962), p. 19.

4. Genesis 12-50 presupposes that this God, El, is the same God as Israel distinctively worships later as Yahweh. It also commonly speaks of El in compound with other expressions in phrases such as El Elyon (El Most High; 14:18-22), El Roi (El

Who Sees Me; 16:13), El Shaddai (El Almighty; 17:1; 28:3; 35:11; 43:14; 48:3), and El Olam (El Eternal; 21:33). Like its equivalent in other Semitic languages (*'il*), Hebrew *'el* can be both a term for deity, like *'elohim* (e.g. Ex 15:2; 20:5), and an actual name for God. It is thus sometimes properly transliterated El, sometimes properly translated 'God' or 'god'. On the significance of the patriarchal religion, and other aspects of the Old Testament, for Christian theology of religions, cf. J. E. Goldingay and C. J. H. Wright, 'Yahweh Our God, Yahweh One: The Oneness of God in the Old Testament', in A. D. Clarke and B. W. Winter (eds.), *One God One Lord: Christianity in a World of Religious Pluralism* (Carlisle: Paternoster; Grand Rapids: Baker, 1992), pp. 43-62. On the relationship between patriarchal religion and later Old Testament faith, cf. R. W. L. Moberly, *The Old Testament of the Old Testament* (Minneapolis: Fortress, 1992).

5. The same question arises in some interpretations of Paul's reference to 'the unknown god' in his speech in Athens, which will be discussed below at the end of the chapter.

6. This point is emphasised as follows by Goldingay and Wright: 'In summary, it can be seen that there are a number of correspondences between Yahweh and El as the Canaanites know him, though these correspondences do not constitute identity. They do not indicate that Canaanite and Israelite faith are identical, or equally valid alternatives depending on where you happen to live… What God began to do with Abram was something of far-reaching significance, even for the Canaanites themselves… The purpose of God's particular action in the history of Israel is ultimately that God, as the saving and covenant God Yahweh, should be known fully and worshipped exclusively by those who as yet imperfectly know him as El. The end result of what God began to do through Abram was of significance for the Canaanites precisely because it critiqued and rejected Canaanite religion.' J. E. Goldingay and C. J. H. Wright, 'Yahweh Our God, Yahweh One: The Oneness of God in the Old Testament', in A. D. Clarke and B. W. Winter (eds.), *One God One Lord: Christianity in a World of Religious Pluralism* (Carlisle: Paternoster; Grand

Rapids: Baker, 1992), pp. 48f. Don Carson's critique of our view on this matter (in *The Gagging of God,* [Leicester: Apollos, 1996], pp. 249-251) picks up on some phraseology that can be misinterpreted and he rightly questions our intent. While it is unquestionably the case that the religion of Israel and that of Canaan had a number of features in common, not only the divine name El, we certainly do not thereby imply that Israel's faith was simply a form of syncretism.

7. For a survey of the sociological distinctiveness of Israel, based on the important work of N. K. Gottwald, *The Tribes of Yahweh: A Sociology of Liberated Israel, 1250-1050 BCE* (London: SCM, 1980), see C. J. H. Wright, 'The Ethical Relevance of Israel as a Society', in *ibid, Walking in the Ways of the Lord: The Ethical Authority of the Old Testament* (Leicester and Downers Grove: IVP, 1996), pp. 147-178.

8. N. K. Gottwald, *The Tribes of Yahweh*, p. 59.

9. J. Verkuyl, *Contemporary Missiology, An Introduction* (Grand Rapids: Eerdmans, 1978), p. 95.

10. Cf. A. Viberg, 'Wakening a sleeping metaphor: A new interpretation of Malachi 1:11', *Tyndale Bulletin* 45.2 (1994) pp. 298-319. Viberg suggests a metaphorical understanding, related to the affirmation of Yahweh as the great king in 1:14, with the implication that as universal king he has the right to the worship of all nations. How much more shameful, therefore, that the worship of his own people, Israel, was so polluted and unacceptable.

11. For a fuller treatment of the Old Testament background to Jesus' teaching about the kingdom of God, see C. J. H. Wright, *Knowing Jesus through the Old Testament* (London: Marshall Pickering, 1992), ch. 5.

12. The alternative rendering is: 'He was the true light who enlightens every person who comes into the world.' But 'coming

into the world' seems unnecessary as an addition to 'every person'. After all, what person does not 'come into the world'? Whereas, it seems perfectly appropriate to take the words as applying to the light itself – i.e. Christ, who was indeed 'coming into the world' in the incarnation.

13. L. Newbigin, *The Open Secret* (London: SPCK, and Grand Rapids: Eerdmans, 1978), p. 196.

14. This point is clearly made in the excellent study of Justin Martyr and his contemporaries by Graham Keith, 'Justin Martyr and religious exclusivism,' *Tyndale Bulletin* 43.1 (1992), pp. 57-80.

15. *Towards a Theology for Inter-Faith Dialogue,* GS 625, C10, Church of England General Synod, Board for Mission and Unity (BMU), (London, 1984).

16. BMU report, paragraph 40.

17. Chris Wright, 'Inter-Faith Dialogue,' *Anvil* 1.3 (1984), pp. 231-258 (p. 244). This article is an extensive review of each section of the BMU report.

18. J. V. Taylor, 'The Theological Basis of Inter-faith Dialogue', *International Review of Mission,* October 1979, pp. 373-384.

19. *Towards a Theology for Inter-Faith Dialogue,* paragraphs 49-50.

20. Carson argues (in *The Gagging of God*) that the text does exclude the possibility of people being saved by Christ without hearing of Christ (which he calls inclusivism, but which I have preferred to regard as a sub-set of exclusivism, as discussed in Chapter 2). Or at least, Carson rightly says that Peter was not addressing the issue of those who might never hear of Jesus, just as he was not addressing the issue of other faiths, and he then questions the view of Pinnock and Sanders that Acts 4:12 does

not rule out the possibility of people being saved without hearing of Jesus. It simply asserts that Jesus is the only means of salvation for anyone. Carson says, 'When to these Jews, many of them doubtless sincere and devout, Peter responds with an exclusive formulation, he quite clearly cannot mean that although salvation, including the final resurrection, is brought about by Jesus and Jesus alone, it is not necessary for devout Jews to recognise that name in order to participate in the resurrection', (p. 305).

Of course he did not mean that, but neither do non-restrictivist exclusivists either. It is of course necessary for those to whom Jesus is intelligibly preached to believe in his name in order to receive salvation. That particular generation of Jews had now witnessed Jesus and heard him preached; there was therefore no other name or way for them to be saved but by the repentance and faith that Peter called for in the name of Jesus. But, as Carson recognises, 'Clearly, this does not *directly* address the fate of those who have never heard,' and who therefore have no possibility of any response to Jesus – positive or negative. Peter was being exclusive in his demand to the Jews, not just because of their heritage that was steeped in biblical revelation, but because they had now been confronted with the Messiah Jesus. Like Paul, Peter would not have been any more flexible in preaching Jesus to Gentile idolaters (to answer a question Carson asks), but that is beside the point – which is to do with those who never hear Jesus preached at all. Jesus must always be preached exclusively! And for precisely the reason given in Acts 4:12. But the question is, as we saw in Chapter 2, is even the possibility of salvation restricted to those to whom Jesus is preached, and thus to the evangelistic obedience and success of the church?

21. This point is another matter of controversy between Pinnock and Sanders on the one hand, and Carson on the other. Pinnock regards Cornelius as on a par with what he calls 'holy pagans' in the Old Testament and goes on to discuss the importance of the two criteria in Acts 10:34-35 – fearing God and doing what is right. Cornelius was 'a believer in God before he became a Christian' (*A Wideness in God's Mercy,* p. 165). According to

Sanders, 'Cornelius was a "saved" *believer* before Peter arrived, but he became a *Christian* and received the fuller blessing of life in Christ only after Peter came' (*No Other Name,* p. 66). Carson draws attention to the point made below that Peter's declaration of God's impartiality (Acts 10:34-35) does not affirm universalism, but only that God welcomes people of any nation, no longer confining the gift of salvation to the Jews. He rightly emphasises that the text stresses that Cornelius received all the blessings of conversion and salvation upon hearing the gospel of Christ. It does not explicitly comment on his salvific status before that moment (*The Gagging of God,* pp. 306-307). Nevertheless, as we discuss below, the text is at pains to describe his response to God in terms that, in an Old Testament context, would imply righteous standing before God (10:2, 4, 22, 31).

22. See Bruce W. Winter, 'On introducing gods to Athens: An alternative reading of Acts 17:18-20, *Tyndale Bulletin* 47.1 (1996), pp.71-90.

23. This reading of the Greek sentence takes it to mean, not: 'The one whom you are actually worshipping but without knowing that you worship him,' but rather, 'The one whom you know you need to worship (because you have an altar to him) but without knowing who and what he is – i.e. the God you really do not know at all.'

24. The mere fact that he quotes them should not, in any case, lead us to imagine that he therefore agreed with everything else these poets and philosophers said. As Carson points out, in his evangelistic preaching he frequently includes quotations from Camus, Sartre, Russell, etc., without for a moment suggesting that he adopts their overall philosophies or that they are 'anonymous Christians'! (*The Gagging of God,* p. 309).

Conclusion

1. Among the most helpful resources to understand these matters are D. Carson, *The Gagging of God: Christianity Confronts*

Pluralism (Leicester: Apollos, 1996); L. Newbigin, *The Gospel in a Pluralist Society* (Grand Rapids: Eerdmans, 1989, and London: SPCK, 1991); A. McGrath, *Bridge-Building: Effective Christian Apologetics* (Leicester: IVP, 1992); J. W. Sire, *The Universe Next Door: A Guide to World Views* (Leicester: IVP, 1977); J. R. Middleton and B. J. Walsh, *Truth is stranger than it used to be: Biblical Faith in a Postmodern Age* (Downers Grove: IVP, and London: SPCK, 1995); M. Eden and D. F. Wells (eds.), *The Gospel in the Modern World: A tribute to John Stott* (Leicester, Downers Grove: IVP, 1991).

For Further Reading

For Further Reading

The following selection of books is for those who wish to study the subject of this book in greater depth. The books listed below contain detailed bibliography.

The following works handle the subject from a broadly exclusivist angle, though with differences over the destiny of the unevangelised (cf. Chapter 2):

N. Anderson, *Christianity and World Religions* (Leicester: IVP, 1970; 2nd rev. ed., 1984)

D. Carson, *The Gagging of God: Christianity Confronts Pluralism* (Leicester: Apollos, 1996)

A.D. Clarke and B.W. Winter, *One God, One Lord: Christianity in a World of Religious Pluralism* (2nd ed. Grand Rapids: Baker, and Carlisle: Paternoster, 1992)

P. Cotterell, *Mission and Meaninglessness: The Good News in a World of Suffering and Disorder* (London: SPCK, 1990)

A. Kirk, *Loosing the Chains: Religion as Opium and Liberation* (London: Hodder and Stoughton, 1992)

H. Netland, *Dissonant Voices: Religious Pluralism and the Question of Truth* (Grand Rapids: Eerdmans, and Leicester: Apollos, 1991).

L. Newbigin, *The Gospel in a Pluralist Society* (London: SPCK, 1989)

L. Newbigin, *The Open Secret: An Introduction to the Theology of Mission* (Grand Rapids: Eerdmans, 1978; 2nd rev. ed. London: SPCK, 1995)

C. Pinnock, *A Wideness in God's Mercy: The Finality of Jesus Christ in a World of Religions* (Grand Rapids: Zondervan, 1992)

J. Piper, *Let the Nations Be Glad: The Supremacy of God in Missions* (Leicester: Apollos, 1993)

J. O. Sanders, *No Other Name: An Investigation into the Destiny of the Unevangelized* (Grand Rapids: Eerdmans, 1992)

V. Ramachandra, *The Recovery of Mission: Beyond the Pluralist Paradigm* (Carlisle: Paternoster, 1996)

The following present an inclusivist viewpoint:

G. D'Costa, *Theology and Religious Pluralism* (Oxford: Blackwell, 1986)

G. D'Costa, *Christian Uniqueness Reconsidered* (Maryknoll, Orbis, 1990)

The writings of pluralist theologians are very diverse and prolific. However, the following provide a survey of their position:

D. Cohn-Sherbok (ed.), *Many Mansions: Interfaith and Religious Intolerance* (London: Bellew, 1992)

J. Hick, *An Interpretation of Religion: Human Responses to the Transcendent* (London: Macmillan, 1989)

J. Hick and P. F. Knitter, *The Myth of Christian Uniqueness* (Maryknoll:Orbis, 1987, and London: SCM, 1988)

P. Knitter, *No Other Name: A Critical Survey of Christian Attitudes Towards the World Religions* (Maryknoll: Orbis, and London: SCM, 1985). This book advocates pluralism, but is very thorough in its presentation of the other main positions in the debate.

On the uniqueness of Jesus in the light of his own Scriptures, see:

C. Wright, *Knowing Jesus through the Old Testament* (London: Harper Collins, 1992, and Downers Grove: IVP, 1995)

Index

Index